CW00525702

Exciting Books About the Oregon Trail

The Oregon Trail Diary of Twin Sisters Cecelia Adams and Parthenia Blank in 1852. Ed. by Bert Webber. The only known diary written by twins who took turns writing along the way. $7.50.

The Oregon Trail Diary of James Akin in 1852. Ed. by Bert Webber. Written by teen-age boy. Includes genealogy. $7.50

The Oregon & Applegate Trail Diary of Welborn Beeson in 1853. Written by teen-age boy. Ed. by Bert Webber. $7.50W

The Oregon & Overland Trail Diary of Mary Louisa Black in 1865. Via Barlow Road. Ed. by Bert Webber. Includes genealogy. $7.50

The Oregon & California Trail Diary of Jane Gould in 1862 Articulate report of Indian massacre. Ed. by Bert Webber $7.50

The Oregon Trail Diary of Edward Evans Parrish in 1844. Very early diary.Ed. by Bert Webber. Includes genealogy. $7.50

> Our Best Oregon Trail Diary Deal: Includes all six diaries, special genealogist's Index; Color Wall Map of Oregon and other trails. Ideal for schools and libraries. Value: $60.   Special "Deal" Price: $48.95

Indians Along the Oregon Trail; The Tribes of Nebraska, Wyoming, Idaho, Oregon and Washington Identified. Bert Webber, M.L.S. Historical essays; facts; "also-known-as" tribal names; language groups, populations – periodically updated. (Encyclopedic). $17.95

The Oregon Trail Memorial Half-Dollar 1926-1939. Bert Webber. America's most distinctive commemorative 50¢ coin was idea of Ezra Meeker, the Oregon Trail's greatest promoter. $4.95

The Old Emigrant Trail; Story of the Lost Trail to Oregon (The Oregon Trail). Introduction and edited by Bert Webber. This was written in 1915 by Ezra Meeker. Now has pictures, map, added. $7.50

The Search For Oregon's Lost Blue Bucket Mine; The Stephen Meek Wagon Train of 1845. Chas. S. Hoffman w/Bert Webber. $12.95

Ezra Meeker; Champion of the Oregon Trail. Bert and Margie Webber. Meeker started trail preservation in 1906 so we can enjoy it today. Includes 98 original Meeker-made photographs. $10.95

Flagstaff Hill on the National Historical Oregon Trail. James R. Evans w/Bert Webber. Only book to include thorough history of exploration that led to development of the Oregon Trail. $12.95

"OUR BOOKS ARE HISTORICALLY ACCURATE AND FUN TO READ"

Shipping costs: Add $2.00 first book, 75¢ each extra book

Books Are Available Through All Independent Book Stores or By Mail from Publisher.

Send stamped, self-addressed envelope to speed copy of latest catalog to you.

WEBB RESEARCH GROUP, PUBLISHERS
P.O. Box 314 Medford, OR 97501

➔Prices and availability may change without notice.

DIARY OF TWIN SISTERS

Markers for Parthenia Blank (left) and Cecelia Adams (right) on same monument in Mountain View Cemetery, Hillsboro, Oregon. The Blank's home in Hillsboro. Pictures made in February 1994.

THE OREGON TRAIL DIARY OF TWIN SISTERS, CECELIA ADAMS AND PARTHENIA BLANK IN 1852

Illustrated With Pictures, Map

The Unabridged Diary
with Introduction and
Contemporary Comments by
BERT WEBBER

WEBB RESEARCH GROUP

Address All Inquiries to the Publisher:
WEBB RESEARCH GROUP
Books About the Oregon Country
P. O. Box 314
Medford, Oregon 97501

LIBRARY OF CONGRESS CATALOGING IN PUBLICATIONS DATA

Adams, Cecelia, 1829-1867.
    The Oregon Trail diary of twin sisters Cecelia
Adams and Parthenia Blank in 1852 : the unabridged
diary / with introduction and contemporary comments
by Bert Webber.
        p.   cm.
Includes biographical references.
ISBN 0-936738-48-0 : $7.50
    1. Oregon Trail. 2. Overland journeys to the Pac-
ific. 3. West (U.S.)—Description and travel, 1848-
1860. 4. Oregon—History—To 1859. 5. Adams, Cecelia,
1829-1867—Diaries. 6. Blank, Parthenia, 1829-1915—
Diaries. 8. Women pioneers—Oregon trail—Diaries. I.
Blank, Parthenia, 1829-1915. II. Webber, Bert. III.
Title.
F880.A19   1990
917.804'2 —dc20   90-12057
                                              CIP

---

iv

Table of Contents

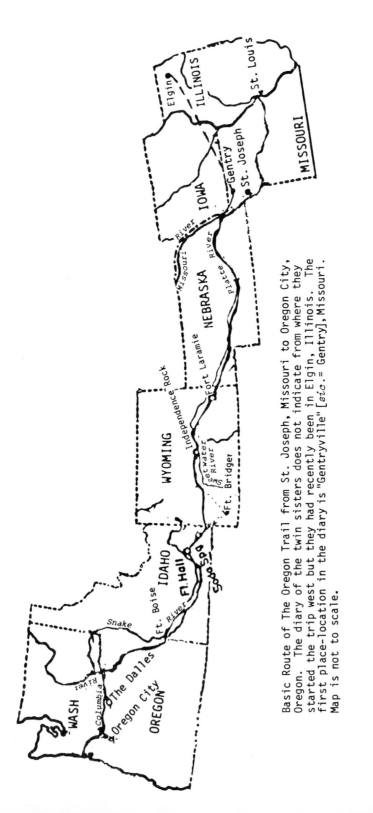

Basic Route of The Oregon Trail from St. Joseph, Missouri to Oregon City, Oregon. The diary of the twin sisters does not indicate from where they started the trip west but they had recently been in Elgin, Illinois. The first place-location in the diary is "Gentryville" [*sic*.= Gentry],Missouri. Map is not to scale.

Dedication

It is probably safe to say that the women who accompanied their men half way across the continent along the Oregon and other trails undoubtedly had little idea what they were getting into before they left. True, there were a few "guide books" but these mostly informed readers where the watering holes and best grass might be found, as well as stated distances between stops. There were some warnings about Indian trouble. Because there was risk of sickness, many women came prepared with medicines and notes on when and how to use them.

Women pitched in and handled all the housekeeping and allied chores along the way. Some drove wagon and chased after strayed cattle. None but the ill rode in the wagon and even they still had the daily work to attend as the women were, along with the men, part of the team. With the men busy with the heavy work, it also fell mostly to women to scrounge the firewood. In the plains area, where there were no trees, or where others before had used all the wood, it was the women who fetched the buffalo chips along the way to use as fuel. Chips make a fast, hot fire over which the women made coffee and boiled beans, baked biscuits and bread.

Further, it was the women who attended the needs of the children, some women stopping along the way to give birth. And it was usually the women who made the simple and minimal preparations for burying the dead. In this

The photograph of the lady of the plains with the load of prairie chips is reported to have appeared in many publications in the 1890's. The print is titled, "Independence on the Plains—Gathering Chips." The Kansas State Historical Society has identified the chip-picker as Ada McCall who, with her mother, Polly McCall, were fetching chips when Polly took the picture near their place near Garden City, Kansas. A very large reproduction of this picture is framed and on exhibit at the National End of the Oregon Trail Interpretative Center in Oregon City, Oregon.

diary we find Cecelia writing (July 2) about stopping for a burial which she describes then:

> We sung a hymn and had a prayer. O!
> It is so hard to leave friends in
> this wilderness

Recognizing the role of women in all aspects of the overland pioneer movement of the nineteenth century, Webb Research Group dedicates this edition of the "twins" diary to the women who headed west along the trails. Many of these women were the "possibility thinkers" of their time who looked forward to new opportunities in a new land. []

Introduction

For many years, decades in fact, just about everyone who came in contact with this diary believed it was the writing of Cecelia Emily McMillen Adams. This belief was apparently pegged to the statement made by George H. Himes, Secretary of the Oregon Pioneer Association, when the Association published the diary in its *Transactions of the Thirty-Second Annual Reunion* in 1904. But now we know there were two writers covering the daily events of this long walk over the plains and across the mountains between Illinois and Oregon.

Cecelia was married to a young physician, Dr. William Adams, who had recently completed his medical studies at Oberlin College in Ohio. The wedding was on June 30, 1849 in Elgin, Illinois, just four months past the bride's twentieth birthday. She had been born in Lodi, New York February 16, 1928 one of twin daughters of Joseph and Ruth McMillen.

The second writer was her sister Parthenia. Parthenia had married Mr. Stephen Blank, a cabinet maker, on November 9, 1850 in St. Charles, Illinois. The weddings of the twins were about eighteen months apart and the two towns, Elgin and St. Charles are observed on today's highway map to be about ten miles apart. These towns are west of Chicago. We do not know the details of their early lives.

In physical stature the twins appeared to be "rather short"—maybe five feet two or three inches. We have not located any references as

to their looks other than to their height. Dr.
Adams, writing many years later (see Appendix)
recalled:

> They were rather short, and in short
> dresses, looked shorter, and when we
> took the short steamboat ride from the
> Cascades [on the Columbia River] to
> Portland, a lady asked my brothers wife
> if those little girls mother was with
> them.

Adams revealed what details we know about
the twins in a letter he wrote to George Himes
on June 1, 1905. He pointed out that while Cecelia

> was a born musician, Artist and teacher
> and worker too, her twin sister was just
> like her [in looks] but very different—
> taciturn, but never gloomy, never sang
> nor played on instruments—had good taste
> but no ambition in art—never taught nor
> wanted to—steady, earnest, cheerful
> work[er].

The McMillan family had apparently been en-
couraged to emigrate to Oregon by the older
brother of the twins, James H. McMillan. He
had made the trip in 1845 and settled at Portland. The 1852 trek included the father of the
girls, Joseph McMillan, a millwright. His
three younger children and his wife (Ruth)
stayed in Illinois. As we learn from the letter of 1905, Doctor Adams and Cecelia had fond
feelings for each other for some time. As the
physician had taken board in her father's tavern, she and the young man saw each other reg-
ularly. When the McMillans decided to move to
Oregon, Cecelia apparently knew about it before her husband. He wrote:

> When, after three years, she asked
> me to come with her to Oregon, I had to
> come. Then with her sister, Mrs. Blank
> and husband—then her father and brother
> Frank, then my bro[ther] Calvin and his

wife who was a cousin of Mrs. Ralph
Greer, all concluded to come, and into
the land of Oregon we came, all safer
and wiser.

This trip took from mid-May through the last
week in October. By contrast, one can drive this
distance in four and one-half days or fly it in
four hours. As the 1852-way was long, hard, dusty,
windy, wet, caused bone-weariness in the stout-
est of souls, homesickness crept in. Cecelia '
broke some of the stress by playing her accordian in the evenings. She laments about not being
able to go to church on Sundays. She is in tor-
ment on learning that her woolen dress had been
left out one night and the oxen ate it. Did she
suffer from migraine headaches? She records two
times of being sick with headache and could not
even sit up.

These young women seemed very much in love
with their men. Parthenia and Stephen's mar-
riage was only a year-and-a-half old when the
party became emigrants on the long trail to
Oregon. Except when they were ill or when the
team was too weak, they walked all the way,
about 2,200 miles. As recorded, when camped
for the night, the two couples slept in the
same wagon, maybe under it, on hot summer nights.
Privacy, which young marrieds seek and need, was
not to be had unless a couple left the train
and wandered away in the wilderness now and then.
They did this as readers will discover. And the
girls sought togetherness and also took side
trips for they were the best of friends. How
they handled themselves on an encounter with
Indians brings a moment of terror.

Many diarists, in fact most, and usually
the men writers, take pains to be direct when
they record the facts of the trip. Their near-
daily record of hard facts provide almost bor-
ing lack of detail. Men write about the grass,
often none; the water, often bad or none; and
the lack of firewood. Diaries by women, on
the other hand, present much more detail. Even
though the stark realities about the grass,
water and wood are there, often almost daily,
many women diarists bring in peripheral obser-
vations which lighten the reading. The twins
mention flowers, trail conditions, wind, gen-

eral and specific comments on many matters.

Nearly as often as there is entry about grass, water and wood, the twins talk about dust. As recorded in another diary:

> The dust is even worse than Indians, storms, or winds, or mosquitoes, or even wood ticks! ...dust...if I could just have a bath!
>
> *The Oregon & California Trail Diary of Jane Gould in 1862* (1987—Webb Research Group)

The emigration of 1852 was very deadly when is came to deaths by cholera along the trail. Some students of the emigration, with interests in the mortality, claim "not less than 5,000 persons died on the route in 1852." (Himes, 1908 *Transactions*) Jane D. Kellogg, in *Transactions* (1913) reported:

> All along the road up the Platte River was a graveyard; almost any time of day you could see people burying their dead; some places five or six graves in a row, with board head signs; it was a sad sight. No one can realize unless he has seen it.

The train in which the twin sisters were a part, stayed out of many of the usual camping places as the earlier pioneers' animals had eaten all or most of the grass. Had they frequented these camp grounds, they would have encountered even more graves than they write about.

In the diary is mention of "nooning." This was the mid-day stop and it was not necessarily at the stroke of twelve. What is today a "lunch" break, was the major meal of the day, "dinner" in this period. During this stop many of the chores were done which included greasing wagon wheels, laundry, advance baking. There was no set length of time for this stop. On some occasions, the break lasted until the following morning. As we shall read, some of the "stay-

where-we-are" delays were necessary as the grass
was particularly good and the animals needed all
the food and rest they could get.

Although Cecelia and Parthenia had an excellent command of the written language, there are
variences in spelling. We have left these as we
found them. Likewise, we have not changed any
of the text but at times, to clarify a point,
or to fill in an obviously missing word, we
use [square brackets] for these instances.

The emigration of 1852 appears to have
been the peak year for the westward movement
over the long trail to Oregon and California.
In that year an estimated 40,000 people moved
along the ruts at an average speed of 2 miles
per hour. In reality, if one had a breakdown,
one was not truly stranded, for another train
would be along with a few minutes. Cecelia
wrote on June 27, "We can see emigrants as far
as the eye can reach." In the Kerns diary,
when near Fort Kearny on June 2, is declared,
"I believe I can count 5,000 wagons this
evening."

The original diary is in the vault of the
Oregon Historical Society but has become frag-
ile over the years to the point where handling
it—even making copy-machine duplications—is
no longer allowed. Also in the vault is the
letter mentioned earlier from Dr. William Adams.
The editor has had a copy of the letter for
some time and recently, the society provided a
typed copy of it for our use here. We very
much appreciate the friendliness and help of
the Oregon Historical Society.

I am indebted to Anne Billeter, head of
the Reference Department of Jackson County
Library in Medford for assistance. While on

14

one of her own field trips, she went to Forest
Grove and Hillsboro areas seeking buriel sites
and newspaper clippings to aid this project.

Our friend, Karen Bolz Cramer, an executive
secretary, finds time to help with the typing
on this and other diaries. Her forebears came
west over the trails. She says the pleasure in
typing these works reminds her of the signifi-
cant role women played in the settling of the
Oregon country. I thank Karen Cramer warmly
for her friendship, interest and professional-
ism.

To my wife, Margie, I am especially indebted. She is loving—with blue pencil in hand—
cheerful—as she uses the blue pencil—smiles
while listening to readings checking for "flow
of the language."

If I have missed anyone who assisted even
in the slightest way, that oversight is uninten-
tional.

Bert Webber, MLS
Central Point, Oregon

Note: When we determined there were two people
who wrote this diary, we decided to print
the diary in a manner allowing a reader to see
at a glance which woman was writing. We have
accomplished this by using different type faces.

At the start of the diary, which incidentally
starts in the middle of a sentence—the earlier
pages are lost—we identify [Parthenia] with
her name in [brackets] and the use of this type.
Not until [Cecelia] takes up pen, do we change.
Readers will observe that Parthenia does all
the writing until June 5 when Cecelia makes a
two-sentence entry. There does not seem to
be any schedule of when the recording would
change hands, it just occurs.

Getting Started

[**Parthenia**]...behind us. Stayed where we were
for 3 hours. Started on. Had hard rain [and]
hail storm. [This] made the roads bad and we
soon camped. Made 14 miles.

Wesnesday, May 19. Found we were on the road
to St. Joseph instead of the Mormon trace
[trail]. Passed through Gentryville* [Gentry
County on Grand River in Missouri] about noon.
Here we had a prairie to cross 15 miles without water, stayed till sunset and went on about
4 miles and encamped on the Prairie carrying
our wood with us. Made 18 miles.

Thursday, May 20. Traveled about 6 miles on
the road to St. J. then took the Savannah
state road and had rare fun in crossing some
of the state mud holes for they beat anything
we had before seen. Encamped on the bank of
the [Little] Platte [river then] forded near
Hunt's Mill. Made 20 miles.

Friday, May 21. Commenced raining soon after
we started and continued to rain all day
mostly. Went on to Ogle's Mill on the [__?__]
River 102 [?] which we forded and camped.
Bought 200 lbs. of flour and 4 bushels meal.
Made 5 miles.

Saturday, May 22. [We] started today and it
soon began to rain but did not continue more
than 2 hours. After traveleing about 7 miles

---
* Parthenia is probably referring to Gentry, as "Gentryville" is well out of the
line of march—Gentryville being only about 30 miles north of the Arkansas line.

we came upon the road leading from Savanna [Missouri] to the [Council] Bluffs. Passed through Newark and crossed the Nottaway [Nodaway] River by ferry. Made 12 miles. Could find no grass for our cattle and as it was near dark we tied them up and stayed till morning.

Sunday, May 23. [We] started for good food and encamped about 3 miles from the river on a Prairie and had first-rate grass. Here we stayed all day. Made 3 miles.

Monday, May 24. Started early. Had rough roads, bad, dry and very hilly. Found some gooseberries and had them at supper. Calvin discovered a litter of young skunks but afterwards found they were calves [*sic*.—probably cavies=guinea pigs]. Reached the Missouri bottom about noon and traveled under the bluff the rest of the day. Made 18 miles.

Tuesday, May 25. Crossed the Little Tarkio and then left the bottom and traveled over hills till we came to the Big Tarkio then took the mud for it. O dear! for about 1/2 mile. Had some rain in the morning and roads not very good. Level ground is not known here. Made 20 miles.

Wednesday, May 26. Had rain all last night and the roads [were] bad in consequence. Traveled slowly till afternoon when we came to the town of Lynden. Here we found roads that had been traveled more and were very good and soon came again into the Missouri bottom, and had good level roads for the rest of the day. Here we got our first sight of the Mo. River and encamped in sight of it on the banks of the Niskinabotany [Nishnabotna] which we crossed on a bridge. Made 17 miles.

Thursday, May 27. Started early and traveled up the bottom for about 6 miles. Paid 25 cents for traveleing the length of a ferry boat across a slough and then up the bluff again. Today we left the state of Missouri and entered Iowa. From this time we found but little bad roads. Mostly prairie, and timber scarce. Passed near the town of Sidney. Made [18 miles].

Friday, May 28. Roads still good. Traveled 17 miles.

Saturday, May 29. Passed through Coonville and crossed Keg Creek. Today we came upon the Mormon trace and traveled about 3 miles on it and encamped on Pony Creek about 5 miles from Kanesville. Made 20 miles.

Sunday, May 30. In the morning found Esquire Hewitt from Dundee [Illinois. He] informed us that our company was encamped about a mile ahead of us. Hitched up our team and started about 11 o'clock but when we got there they had left, but we passed on and soon found them camped again in a field on the Missouri bottom about 2 miles from Kanesville. Of course we camped too.

Monday, May 31. Went to Kanesville and did some trading.

Tuesday, June 1. We did the same.

Wednesday, June 2. The same.

Thursday, June 3. Started and went to the ferry, the Old Trader's Point, Council Bluffs Post Office 6 miles.

18

Friday, June 4. This is a day long to be re-
membered for hard work. Paid $1.00 per wagon
and 25 cents per yoke of oxen for the privilege of ferrying ourselves over the Missouri
in a flat boat which took us all day and till
after dark. Made 1 mile. Our company now
consists of 6 wagons, one of which is bound
for California. A great many Mormons are
starting for the Salt Lake.

[At this point in the diary is a poem signed by
Cecelia.]:

> Home
>   what so sweet!
> So beautiful on Earth! Oh! So Rare
>   as kindred love and family repose:
>   The busy world
> With all the tumult and stir of life
>   Pursues its wonted course; on pleasures some
> And some on commerce and ambition bent
>   And all on happiness, while each one loves
> With nature's holiest feelings. One sweet spot
>   And calls it home. If sorrow is felt
> There it seems through many bosoms and a smile
>   And if disease intrudes
> The sufferer finds
>   Rest on the breast beloved.

[**Parthenia**] Saturday, June 5. Proceeded up a
pretty hilly road and but little of interest
occurred. Made 15 miles.

[**Cecelia**] Just commenced keeping guard [at
night]. Found some strawberries today.

[**Parthenia**] Sunday, June 6. Proceeded on.
At noon when we stopped for dinner the cattle
took a stampede for about a mile, cause
unknown. At night, as we were about to encamp,
they took another with the wagons but did not

do much damage and were soon stopped.

[Cecelia] Last night my clothes got out of the
wagon and the oxen ate them up and I consider
I have met with a great loss as it was my
woolen dress.

[Parthenia] Monday, June 7. Nothing of much
interest occurred today except a cold night
last night. Ferried across the Elkhorn and
forded Rawhide and reached the bank of the
Platte. Made 24 miles. While we were crossing the Elkhorn it rained and hailed very hard.

[Cecelia] [Writing on the same day]. Today we
saw 4 Indian's graves. They were quite open.
I could see 2 buffalo robes within which had
probably been wrapped around the body. They
were buried on the surface of the earth and
mounds erected over them and an opening had
been made in the side probably by emigrants.
As we were looking at them we saw 4 Indians
coming towards us on horseback which caused us
to be leaving. They had been stealing sheep
from the emigrants.

[Parthenia] Tuesday, June 8. Proceeded on up
the Platte. Caught a few small fish. Roads
fine and boundless level prairie. Made 17 miles.

[Cecelia] Wednesday, June 9. We are all very
glad to get on our clocks [probably cloaks]
and overcoats and mittens this morning. It is
so very cold. North wind blows very hard.
Noon here we find a new made grave. On the
headboard is inscribed "D Herer died May 28th
1852. Aged 5 years." Today we met several
teams on their way back. We made no inquiries
as they had the small pox. We also saw some
Mormons on their way back. They said the road

was good and no Indians on our way as far up as Ft. Laramie. Made 19 miles.

Thursday, June 10. Hard south wind for several days followed up the Loup Fork. This is a branch of the Platte a very rapid stream filled with sand bars. Find a few wild roses and yellow daisies. Tonight we encamped on a beautiful spot with plenty of wood and grass. One of our oxen has become very lame. Timber is generally very scarce. Today we saw 2 new graves. On the headboard was written with a pencil "Mary Morris aged 19 and M C Morris aged 9 yrs." We saw good clothing scatter around which caused us to think they had died with some contagious disease. Here we did some washing. Made 18 miles.

Friday, June 11. S. W. [south west wind]. Took an early start this morning. P[arthenia] and myself walked on several miles. We have very cold nights and not very warm days which makes it fine for our cattle. 12 o'clock stopped for dinner. This is all the time I get to write or read. The horse flies are very bad today. I never saw such large ones and so many of them before. The boys are all laying under the wagons asleep. Today crossed Looking Glass Creek, Beaver Creek, Plumb Creek, and Ash Creek. We find quite a number of dead oxen and horses. Encamp'd on the Loup Fork bottom tonight, We could hear the Indians but did not see any. Made 20 miles.

Saturday, June 12. W. W. [west wind]. Quite warm today with a cool breeze. We came to an old deserted Indian village. We think by the looks of the land that it has been cultivated in a few places. Found some Cedar for the first time. The soil is very sandy. Grass is

very good here. Cottonwood is the principal
timber on these rivers. See no buffalo yet.
This is a beautiful part of the country, very
level. We have some good neighbors in our
company. Encamped for the night on the Loup
Fork. Had to go 2 miles for wood. Made
19 miles.

Sunday, June 13. W. wind very hard. This is
a lovely morning but has the appearance of
rain which made us very anxious to ford the
river so we started on. Found it rather dangerous crossing on account of quicksand. Mr.
Miller's wagon came very near going down. P
and self waded through, took father for our
pilot. We had a grand time as we had to
follow down the river half-a-mile so that we
traveled nearly a mile in the water. We feel
all the better for our ducking. It took us
nearly all day, but got across safe at last.
Seems but little like the Sabbath. Find a few
strange flowers. Made 6 1/2 miles. Think[ing]
of anne [their 14 year-old-sister ·who was
still at home in Illinois with their mother]
as it was her birthday. [Their father was a
part of this wagon train.]

Monday, June 14. Very hard W. wind. Took an
early start this morning calculating to stop
and rest our teams as soon as we come to good
grass which our guide book says will be 2 or
3 days' travel. Here we find toads with horns
and long tails. They are about 3 inches long
and very slender and tails as long as the body.
They are spotted white, yellow and brown. Can
run as fast as a man and very wild. Mosquitoes
annoy us very much and sometimes the air seems
to be filled with large bugs. Dust is very
troublesome, roads good. Water scarce, grass
poor, no timber. This afternoon we passed 7

new-made graves, one had 4 bodies in it and to all appearances they were laid on the top of the ground and the dirt thrown over them. Most of them were aged people. It was written on some of the headboards that they died with the cholera. We find good bed clothes and clothing of all kinds but do not pretend to touch [any] one of them. Encamped for the night on the wide prairie creek. Find good grass and water but no wood but we brought wood with us as our guide [or guide*book*—not clear which] directed us to do. Made 23 miles.

Tuesday, June 15. N. wind, quite cool, rained very hard last night which was acceptable to us. Did not take an early start this morn as we do not calculate to drive any great distance today as our teams are getting very tired and our lame ox is no better. I had the sick headache last night and do not feel able to sit up much today. Have a good bed in the wagon. Our folks had a new milk cow today. Encamped on the Platte. Poor wood and grass. Rained all day which makes it very disagreeable getting supper tonight. Made 11 1/2 miles.

Wednesday, June 16. Wind N. E. Rainy this morning, very disagreeable getting breakfast. We concluded to go on slowly until we find a better camping place. A man died this morning with the cholera in a company ahead of us. Find prickly pear. All the wood we find today is quaking asp which is miserable for fuel. Have no wild game yet, altho our boys are on the chase most of the time. Passed 11 new graves. Crossed Weed Creek, encamped 1 mile from the Platte. Poor wood and miserable water [but] good grass. Made 13 miles. Elected officers tonight [in our company].

Thursday, June 17. Very warm and sultry. Concluded to stay and do our washing by taking
our clothes down to the river we can wash very
well. Another man died near us this morning.

The doctor gets some practice. Henry is quite
unwell today but as a general thing we are
blessed with excellent health and good spirits.
At 3 o'clock concluded to pick up and go a
little ways as we shall have a long drive tomorrow. Did a large washing, had the hardest
water I ever saw. Oxen getting better. [We
had] brought our wood and water with us [but]
found water enough for our cattle. Made 4
miles. Had a new milk cow today.

Friday, June 18. Warm and sultry. Took an
early start this morning. Our company at the
present consists of 8 wagons, 16 men and 10
ladies, besides children. A large company
passes us today from Kane Co[unty] Illinois—
Elgin Dundee and St. Charles all horse teams.
They seemed like our own folks. Another man
died near us today and an old lady 56 years
old. The doctors think that they drank poison
water out of a spring near here.

[Parthenia] Here we find lockspur and also a
very pretty dark red flower, strangers to us.
They resemble the moss rose. This afternoon
we had a very heavy shower accompanied with
hail and hard wind. We have passed 21 new-
made graves today. It makes it seem very
gloomy to us to see so many of the emigrants
buried on the plains. Made 18 miles.

Saturday, June 19. Very warm. Took an early
start. Crossed a very deep ravene with steep
banks which was entirely dry. Our boys have
been hunting all the forenoon. Just returned

with a buffalo covered with feathers about the
size of a prairie hen, is all the game we have
yet. Passed 13 graves today. We just met a
train from Fort Laramie going to St. Joseph
with the mail, but would not wait for us to
write any letters so mother missed of one this
time. Encamped on Elm Creek, a very beautiful
spot. It seems too bad to see such pretty
places uninhabited. We see snipe, turkey
buzzards and a few blackbirds. We [have] seen
no Indians yet. The express men tell us we
shall find none until we get to Fort Laramie.
Made 16 miles. At noon father made us a good
cup of tea.

Sunday, June 20. This is a beautiful morning.
Very warm [and] did not expect to travel any
today. A few sweet birds are singing and all
nature seems to be praising their Maker. I
cannot help thinking of our dear home today.
I think I see them going to the house of God
to worship there. 0! what a blessed privilege.
Here on this wide prairie we seldom hear the
voice of prayers. But I trust a spirit of
prayer and praise is felt in all most every
heart. We have great reason to be thankful
for the many blessings and mercies that daily
attend us through dangers both seen and unseen
the hand of God has directed us, and while we
see so many continually falling around us, we
still live in the enjoyment of good health and
spirits. "Bless the Lord oh my soul. Let all
that is within me bless his holy name." It
seems best for us to travel today as we shall
be obliged to stop again in a day or two. We
have more time for reading and meditation when
we are traveling than we do when we stop and
spend a day. We have so much to do when we
stop it keeps us busy all day. Passed 10
graves. We lost our Guide Book on Saturday

which caused us to go much farther today than
we expected. We find a great many sink holes.
They are round hollow places in the ground
Filled with alkali water. If they dry up it
leaves the earth covered with saleratus. We
have to guard our cattle from them all the
time. Our hunting boys ran after them with
their guns prepared but they ran towards them
so fast it frightened them away. They were
most too anxious. We encamped on the prairie,
carried our wood with us besides picking up
buffalo chips for the fire. Made 16 miles.

Monday, June 21. Wind N. E. Very pleasant.
Took an early start. Mr. Stoel [John Stowell
and wife Margaret and family from Tennessee]
came back to us last night. Has not been with
us before for 5 weeks or more. [We] are glad
to have our friend come back with us again.
Very high wind this afternoon which makes it
very bad traveling. Today we can see teams on
the other side of the Platte. That is the road
that James [H. McMillen, our oldest brother]
traveled [in 1845]. Today 5 men direct from
Oregon [on their way east visited and waited].
They gave us the privilege of writing home.
Last night we had music and dancing. It makes
it seem quite like home to hear the accordian
which Cecelia plays most every evening. Not
very good roads. Made 20 miles.

[Cecelia] Tuesday, June 22. Cool and pleasant.
Stephen [Blank] is quite unwell today. Some
of our boys are hunting today. Some men from
Oregon came along today on their way back to
the states [and] tell us we shall find plenty
of grass ahead and no Indians. We sent two
letters home by them. One of them said he was
acquainted with James [McMillen]. Passed 7
graves. If we should go by all the camping

Unidentified grave on the Oregon Trail. The Oregon-California Trails Association headquartered in Independence, Missouri, is making a concerted effort to identify and mark as many graves as possible.

grounds we should see five times as many graves as we now do. At noon it rained very hard and continued so all afternoon very hard wind. Had rather a disagreeable time getting supper. Our [buffalo] chips burn rather poor as they are so wet. It seems like a winter night it is so very cold. Made 14 miles.

Wednesday, June 23. This is a gloomy morning. It rained so much last night. Today we come to some bluffs for the first time. Sandy roads and hard drawing. Good grass. Find some wood, very poor. Take some with us. Poor water. Crossed Skunk Creek. Encamped for the night with no wood or water excepting what we had with us. Passed 21 graves. Here we find a white poppy but they are so covered with thorns that we cannot pick them. Made 18 miles.

Thursday, June 24. Wind N. E. Very cold indeed this morning. Took an early start. Found some

good looking springs but dare not use any of
the water. Roads good, very dandy. We can
see teams on the other side of the Platte the
road that brother James traveled on. But our
road is much the best as there are so many
bluffs on the other road. Passed 18 graves.
We met another Oregon train today on their
way back to Iowa. It consisted of men, women
and children. They were packed on horses,
had but one wagon. We inquired if they were
sick of Oregon. They said no—and expected
to go back next spring. They were in such a
hurry they would not stop to talk. Today we
see the last timber for 200 miles so our
Guide [book] says. Made 18 miles.

Friday, June 25. Wind E. This morning. Woke
up and found it raining very hard. We expected
to do our washing here today but it rains so
that we concluded to travel. The roads rather
bad. Use[ing] Platte [River] water. It is a
very muddy stream. We can settle it with alum
so it [becomes] very good. Generally get a
pint of mud out of every pail of water. Today we passed a grave that had been dug open
by the wolves. All we could see of the remains
were the clothes that it had been wrapped up
in. We found the headboard some distance
from the grave, on it was inscribed "Henry
Verdant Aged 52 from Edgar County, Illinois."
Crossed the North Bluff fork. Passed 8
graves. Traveled 4 miles on the bluffs. So
much sand that it is almost impossible to get
over them. Did not find a camping ground
till very late. Mosquitoes very troublesome.
Made 18 miles.

Saturday, June 26. Wind E. Did not start very
early as we overslept ourselves. Have a hard
time getting a fire to cook our breakfast as

everything is so wet. Some of our company had
a regular fight today but all of our folks kept
out of the muss. One or two was knocked down
but no injury done only they are obliged to
leave our company. Find prickly pears in great
abundance. The flowers of one kind resemble
the double yellow hollyhocks and the other kind
resemble the pink china aster. The pink ones
are very beautiful. Passed through another
dog town today. They resemble the fox squarrel
in shape and color. It is almost impossible
to kill one of them. They are so very shy.
Passed some deep ravines. Passed 9 graves.
Very sandy roads. Find some beautiful looking
springs but dare not use the water. Keep near
the Platte. Good grass, no wood. Made 18 miles.

Sunday, June 27. This is a lovely morning [so
we] conclude to stay here today and recruit our
team. They have stood the journey very well
but want some rest. But we find a great deal
to do. P did some washing and I baked bread
and pumpkin and apple pies, cooked beans and
meat, stewed apples and baked suckeyes in
quantities sufficient to last some time.
Besides making Dutch cheese and took every
thing out of the wagons to air. A birth took
place today in one of the companies near us.
It threatened a hard storm this afternoon but
only gave us a few drops and passed on.
Buffalo bones are scattered all over the
plains. We can see emigrants as far as the
eye can reach. I do not see any company that
can get along better than we do. We all take
a great deal of comfort expecially sister P
and myself. We have some jolly times if we
are in the wilderness [walking together away
from the train].

Monday, June 28. South W. Cool and pleasant.

Started early. Roads sandy. Crossed two small
creeks. Stopped for dinner opposite Cedar
Bluffs on the other side of the Platte. Some
of the boys are out on a hunting excursion.
Passed 11 graves. Encamped for the night on
the banks of the Platte. Some little sickness
in some of the companies but we all enjoy good
health which we consider a great blessing.
Made 19 miles.

Tuesday, June 29. Wind W. Last night about
12 o'clock the wind blew a perfect hurricane
which made a scattering among the tents. We
slept in our wagon and it rocked like a
cradle. [We] expected it to go over every
moment altho they were chained down. But it
is very calm this morning. After traveling
some 4 miles of good road we came to some
very high bluffs the highest we have seen yet.
P and myself forded a little stream barefoot
and walked over the bluffs which are a mile
in length. Sand very deep. Passed 10 graves.
Passed the lone tree the only stick of timber
within 200 miles. This is about half way
between. The tops have all been cut off. It
is cedar. We took a few splinters in memory
of it. Encamped on Cassell [castle] Creek.
Passed another dog town. Made 20 miles.
Passed Ash Holler Station, where one man
stays alone.

Wednesday, June 30. W. N. Very pleasant. Last
night had another hard wind and some little
rain. The bluffs look very beautiful on the
other side of the Platte but should not like
to travel over them. Good grass. Passed 10
graves. Find considerable driftwood [along the
high-water line of the river]. Made 22 miles.

Thursday, July 1. Wind S. E. Has the appearance

Chimney Rock, in west-central Nebraska, was a "tower of hope" to emigrants because they could see it many miles in the distance. It grew larger as they approached thus they knew they were making progress even at the average wagon speed of 2 miles per hour.

of a storm. We see antelope very often but our hunters have not caught any thing worth speaking of yet. Have killed two or three yellow rattlesnakes. Large grey wolves are very plenty. They will kill buffalo and the emigrants sometimes lose their cattle. Passed 8 graves. One of the men that left our camp is very sick. One that had a quarrel with his son in law. Made 21 miles.

Friday, July 2. Had a very hard wind last night. The sick man is dead this morning. We stop to see him buried. They wrapped him in bed clothes and laid him in the ground without any coffin. We sung a hymn and had prayer. O! it is so hard to leave friends in this wilderness! Some of the bluffs look like old

Jail Rock, east of Scotts Bluff, Nebraska.
This is near Chimney Rock.

castles. Are in sight of Chimney Rock, can
see it fifty miles off. Passed 8 graves.
Follow on the Platte, very poor grass, quite
warm, travel slowly. Made 16 miles.

Saturday, July 3. Wind westerly. Very pleasant
today. We come to the river opposite Chimney
Rock which has been visible most of the way
for the last 35 miles. It is said to be 3
miles from the opposite side of the river but
on these level prairies we cannot judge much
of distances by the eye. It does not appear
more than half a mile. It consists of a
large square column of clay and sand mixed
together with a base of conical form apparently
composed of sand, round base cone, and appears
as if the column had been set up and the sand
heaped around it to sustain it. It is said to
be 500 feet high but doubt it some. Just back
of it to the south is another structure of the

Scotts Bluff National Monument near Gering and Scotts
Bluff, Nebraska, is visited by thousands of people every
year. Several permanent exhibits are seen including this
covered wagon and its 30-star American flag.

same material which has the appearance of an
Illinois straw stable [shed] and a little to
the west is a cluster which the imagination
can easily make a barn and stacks and which
bears this name. We very much regret that we
could not cross the river and get a closer
view of it but we can see it very distinctly
through our spyglass. I love to look at it
because I know that Brother James [McMillen]
been on it. We see a great many strange looking rock that look like old ruins but I could
not describe them accurately had I time. Made
16 miles today.

Sunday, July 4. Winds westerly. This is a
delightful morning. A few sweet birds are
trying to sing their Maker's praise. Our
thoughts are continuely turning homeward. I
suppose you are all having a sabbath school
celebration today. We would like to take a

sly squint and see what you are doing. This morning met a train from California on their way back to the States. They tell us we shall be rather late [for the season] but little trouble, if any, with the Indians. Seemed much pleased with our new style of dress. To day Henry found an ox that had been left because he was a little lame. [Our men] put some shoes on him and think he will do us a great deal of good. Passed 2 graves. Encamped on the Platte. Made 15 miles.

Monday, July 5. W. W. The wind blows hard every night. Today we see Laramie Peak. It looks like a cloud. It is over 100 miles from here. Roads good. Passed 9 graves. Made 18 miles.

Tuesday, July 6. W. South. Pleasant and cool. Today we come to timber mostly cottonwood. A Mrs. Wilson in our company is quite sick so that we cannot go very fast. Roads very good. Passed 6 graves. Grass rather poor. Has the appearance of a hard storm. Made 9 miles.

Wednesday, July 7. W. W. Last night we had a very hard rain and how hard the wind blew. Our sick woman much better. Started on and commenced raining but it soon passed off and has the appearance of a pleasant day. Passed a tent, where we found one [man] keeping a grocery store. He kept a [stock] of a little of everything but a person must want very bad before paying high prices.

[Parthenia] Roads good most of the day but towards night, sandy. Camped 3 miles below Fort Laramie. Plenty of wood, a great luxury, for it is the first time we have had it for more than 200 miles.

FORT LARAMIE NATIONAL HISTORIC SITE
Originally built in 1834, served as resting place
for trappers, emigrants, now tourists.
The fort is mentioned in most diaries. Those folks
on the south side of the Platte River stopped but
most on the north side merely make mention—did
not cross the river but frequently sent someone to
seek mail. Official U.S. Post Office opened in 1850.

Thursday, July 8. Today we do not travel for we want to do some business at the fort and the women want to wash. A lady is quite (?) today. [We] hope she will be better soon.

[**Cecelia**] Friday, July 9. West wind [today]. Started on very pleasant roads, very sandy. Passed by the fort. Left four letters at the Post Office. Saw some Indians. Found some wild currants—two kinds black and yellow ones. [We] camped on the bottoms of the Platte. Made 14 miles.

Saturday, July 10. S. W. Very cold this morning. Today we come into the Black Hills. They seem to be solid rock and very high and steep covered with pitch pine and cedar. P and I climbed one of them and had as much as we wanted to do to get down, it requires long toe nails to go up and down them. Stopped for dinner but could find nothing for our poor cattle, neither grass nor water. Passed 8 graves. Encamped on the Platte. Poor grass, plenty of wood and water. Made 14 miles.

Sunday, July 11. Very cool wind [and we] started very late. Our road is so up hill then down again. Find some beautiful yellow flowers that resemble the evening beauty and some little bluebells and a white flower resembling the lily and blue larkspurs and the little yellow sunflowers. Find wild sage for the first time. No water and poor grass. Passed 15 graves. [We] camped near the Platte [River]. Made 13 miles.

Monday, July 12. Wind from the north. Cool and cloudy. Started early. Found neither grass nor water until about 5'oclock today. We left an ox as it was so lame, but Henry's ox takes its place. It is now cloudy every afternoon. Passed 5 graves. Poor grass. Made 15 miles.

Tuesday, July 13. W. S. Very pleasant. Henry killed a mountain hen. It resembled a prairie hen but I think superior in flavor is some larger. P and I walked on ahead of the rest of the company some distance. Went down a steep hill [just as] some Indians on horseback came along. We were somewhat frightened [so] we turned back toward our teams. Found the Indians were much nearer than we had expected and so we stood still and looked at them. They looked at us very smilingly with painted faces and [their] long hair hanging down on the back. We passed on and left them there standing gazing at us. Our boys are on a buffalo hunt. Hope they will get one. Well, here they come, each one loaded with buffalo meat. We do not relish it as well as we had expected. It is very much like beef. [We had] good roads. Made 20 miles.

Wednesday-Friday, July 14, 15, 16. Spent this time in resting our teams and in swimming them across the Platte [where] we found excellent grass. Spent our time washing, repairing the wagons and making a new tent. Our boys killed an antelope which we all relish very much. Also caught some nice fish. It is very warm.

Saturday, July 17. Very pleasant this morning. Did not get started very early, it took so long to get our cattle over the river. Find the roads very dandy and hilly. No grass. Passed 3 graves. Encamped on the Platte. Made 14 miles.

Sunday, July 18. W. W. Very pleasant with a good breeze. Think of home a great deal today.

Now and then see a buffalo. No grass on this side of the river. We swim our cattle over every night and back in the morning. We must keep a constant guard by them. Roads very sandy. Encamped for the night on the side of the Platte. Passed 4 graves. Made 16 miles.

Monday, July 19. Wind west. Cool and pleasant. Roads very sandy. Dust very troublesome. We walked most of the day. Passed by 2 graves. The ground is covered with little purple, pink and white daisies. Mosquitoes very annoying. Made 14 miles.

Tuesday, July 20. W. E. Cool breeze. Today met some men from California on the way back to the States. Gave us much encouragement. We have nothing but sand to travel today. We encamped tonight on the Platte for the last time. See plenty of buffalo but can kill none of them. Made 10 miles.

Wednesday, July 21. Winds from east. Concluded to spend the day here and repair the wagons and rest the teams. We do our washing. Find plenty of wild currants. They are very good, but not equal to the tame. Find good grass and water.

Thursday, July 22. W. N. Today passed the ferry where James came over in our road. I have the sick headache today so that I am not able to sit up. Met another train of Oregon men, would not stop to talk with us. The Indians are gathered around us today. They look very savage but we are well prepared for them. We go in large companies. Very good roads. Today we leave the Platte for good. Made 14 miles.

Friday, July 23. W. W. This morning we started at 3 o'clock as we had 15 miles to go without water, and wanted to travel in the çool of the day. Did not stop to get any breakfast for our cattle or ourselves. Passed 7 graves. We encamped tonight on Willows Springs. Find good grass by driving our cattle 2 miles off the road and keep a strict guard. Good water. All keep well. Made 15 miles.

Saturday, July 24. W. W. Very pleasant and warm. Did not start early, as we do not expect to go far. Stopped at noon on Greasewood Creek. Here we will stay until morning. Passed 3 graves. Poor grass, no wood [but] good water. Made 10 miles.

Sunday, July 25. Wind west. This morning we started at 3 o'clock [looking for] good feed. This is a beautiful Sabbath morning. All is still with the exception of the wagons rolling on. We stopped at 8 o'clock to feed [animals] and to get our breakfast. Sand very deep and dust troublesome. [Editor's note: They are now on the Sweetwater River.] Stopped for dinner opposite Independence Rock. It is a great curiosity but we are so tired that we could not go to the top of it. It is nearly covered with names of emigrants. Went on to the Devil's Gate and encamped. This is a great curiosity but we have not the time to visit it [which] we regret very much. Passed 3 graves. Forded the Sweetwater. Made 16 miles.

Monday, July 26. W. W. Cool mornings and evenings but warm and sultry through the day. Find a great many dead cattle. Today passed a Station. Here we traded off a yoke of oxen for a yoke of cows. Our oxen were sorefooted. Passed 3 graves. Roads very sandy. Encamped

INDEPENDENCE ROCK
It rises 193 feet above the valley floor, was resting place used by pioneers due to closeness of Sweet-Water River. Can be climbed easily from side hidden from highway. Wind blows sharply. Wear non-skid shoes. Be alert for pesky Wyoming rattle-snakes near base of rock. (top, left) Bert Webber on the top, August 1987.

Independence Rock was an excellent resting place for emigrants as it was next to the Sweetwater River. The rock can be climbed fairly easily from the east side, rises 193 feet above the valley floor. Wind on top of the rock is nearly always brisk. Hikers should wear non-skid shoes and be alert for pesky Wyoming rattle-snakes near base of the rock. Hundreds of names were scratched in the rock by pioneers.

on the Sweetwater [where we] find good grass. Made 14 miles.

Tuesday, July 27. Very warm. We can see nothing on either side but mountains. Roads very sandy and dust troublesome. Keep on the Sweetwater River. Find gooseberries. They are very sour indeed. Passed 3 graves. Encamped on the river. Made 14 miles.

Wednesday, July 28. East winds. Warm and pleasant. Parthenia and I climbed a very steep rock some 400 to 500 feet high and got very tired indeed. Found a great many names. Today we can see the snow-capped mountains for

the first time. Roads in some places very
bad. Keep[ing along] the Sweetwater River.
Very poor grass. Made 17 miles.

Thursday, July 29. This morning we were obli-
gated to start at 1 o'clock and go 10 miles
before we could find any grass for our cattle.
They had no water or [feed] last night. We
stopped at sunrise and found very good feed
by driving our cattle 2 or 3 miles off. Mr.
Miller is quite sick today, fear he has the
mountain fever. We shall stay here till noon.
We do some washing and baking. Started on at
noon went 6 miles. Encamped on the river near
some willow springs, one of James' camping
grounds (near the river fork). He is 9 days
ahead of us. Very poor grass. Passed 8 graves
within 2 days. Made 16 miles.

Friday, July 30. W. N. Took an early start
this morning. Have some very bad hills to
climb today. Passed some very good springs
and several saleratus lakes last night. One
of the doctor's cows died today. I have kept
an account of the dead cattle we passed and
the number today is 35. We passed a station
here today. We saw plenty of Indians. They
seem very friendly. They were engaged in
dressing some prairie dogs. They had several
little papooses who looked very [cute—?-the
word is not clear but the 1904 printing and
Holmes say the papooses were "cunning." But
the warriors might have looked "cunning"—
probably not the babies—even though Cecelia
has just recorded "They (the Indians) seem
very friendly.]" Some of the Indians were
making moccasins for sale. They trim them
very nice with beads. [We] went on a little
farther and came to another camp. Here there
was a blacksmith shop. We saw but one white

lady here. The men were engaged in playing cards and gambling. Passed 5 graves.

Saturday, July 31. W. W. Cool and pleasant. Did not start very early as we do not expect to go far today. Roads very good. The snow-cap mountains lie directly north of us today. Here we find strawberries and huckleberries, the latter not ripe yet. Encamped at noon. Drive our cattle off 3 miles and get excellent feed. Do some washing. Clouds up and rains this afternoon. Made 12 miles.

[Parthenia] Sunday, Aug. 1. Today we left the waters that flow into the Atlantic and proceed to those of the Pacific. We let our cattle feed till about noon and then started on, for the South Pass, 10 miles distant. It ill comports with the ideas we had formed of a pass through the Rocky Mountains, being merely a vast level sandy plain, sloping a little each way from the summit, and a few

hills, for we could not call them mountains, on each side. Some few snowy peaks in the distance and this is the South Pass through the Rocky Mountains. From the summit we proceeded down a gentle slope to the Pacific Spring and Creek, 3 miles, and encamped for the night. Here we could find no grass except on a deep slough formed by the springs and covered with turf and grass on which a man can stand and shake the ground for several feet around him, it is so soft underneath. Upon this we put our cattle to feed, for it was the only chance, and the sod was so tough they did not break through very much. The Pacific Springs rise in the middle of this, boiling up through the sod, and as cold as ice itself. Made 13 miles. [South Pass: 7,550 elev.]

Monday, Aug. 2. Today we left the springs
for a long pull of 24 miles to Little Sandy
Creek. Crossed Dry Sandy Creek, but it con-
tained no good water, and we made the whole
distance without any. Soon after we started
we met a packtrain from California on their
way home. Came about noon to the forks of the
old Oregon and Salt Lake road. Took the road
to Salt Lake with the intention of going by
Kinney's Cutoff to avoid the desert. [Editor's
note: Many trains followed Sublette, Cutoff
which left the main trail at what became known
as "Parting of the Ways." This cut out the
long trek southward to Fort Bridger then northwest from Fort Bridger to rejoin at the west
end of the Sublette. But the haul over the desert on the Sublette was a real chore. A kind
of half-way effort at avoiding Fort Bridger
as well as the hot desert along the Sublette
was the Kinney Cutoff. To use this route,
emigrants took the Fort Bridger fork along the
Big Sandy River to near where that river joined
the Green River. When cutting acorss between
the two rivers, about 10 miles, one would
arrive at the Green River near where a ferry
operated during high water. When the river was
low, as in August, it was an easy manner to
wade across it. It should be pointed out for
trail purists, there is a Kinney Cutoff as well
as a trail called Alternate Kinney Cutoff. The
Kinney runs along the present-day Farson -
Fontenelle Road for a while but the Alternate
Kinney goes to the ferry site. For clarity,
one might look at Gregory Franzwa's book *Maps
of the Oregon Trail* (see bibliography), pages
148-149.]

[**Parthenia** continues] Reached Little
Sandy River a little before sunset. Found
plenty of good water though somewhat muddy

like the Platte, but no grass for the cattle
it having been all eaten off. We let our cattle
feed as well as they could till dark and then
tied them up to keep them from wandering off
for feed. Hardest time yet. The road today
has been as level as you often find even in
Illinois slightly inclining to the south and

"Parting of the Ways," west-central Wyoming. The trail at left goes to Ft. Bridger. Several short-cuts to the west start here on the right. A marker on Highway 28 mentions "Parting of the Ways," alas the marker is in wrong place. The fork in the trail is about two miles west and about three miles to the north—not visible from the highway. Four-wheel-drive vehicles can make it on unimproved road but the chuckholes are bad.

west. You hardly believe yourself among the mountains. Old Cataraugus [Cattaraugus—some hills about 40 miles south of Buffalo, N.Y.] beats it all hollow. Made 21 miles.

Tuesday, Aug. 3. We started early for the Big Sandy in hopes of finding better grass, but did not find it much better.

[Cecelia] Stopped here at noon and concluded to stay a day or more as Mr. Miller is very sick. Find good feed by going 3 miles off. We have very heavy dews this side of the pass. Made 11 miles.

Wednesday, Aug. 4. Pleasant. We shall stay here today as Mr. Miller is not able to ride.

It rains some. We meet a great many Mormons. [They] want us to go to Salt Lake [City] with them].

Thursday, Aug. 5. Our sick man is better and we make a move this morning in good spirits. Road rather sandy but level. Encamped on the Big Sandy River. Made 17 miles.

Friday, Aug. 6. This morning we leave the Big Sandy for good. Have very sandy roads. Met 3 men from Oregon on their way to the States. We see no water from morning till night. Encamped tonight on the long-looked-for Green River, a very muddy stream, the water looks red. Had a very heavy wind in the afternoon, but very warm through the day. Saw no flowers today. Made 17 miles.

Saturday, Aug. 7. Very warm this morning. We ferry over Green River. Have to pay $3 per wagon. Here is a station 3 or 4 white men and a few Indians. Passed but 8 graves within a week. Traveled over rough roads. Made 16 miles.

Sunday, Aug. 8. Very cold this morning, need overcoats and mittens. Father was very sick all night, is some better this morn. We take a late start on his account. This afternoon we climb some mountains, worse than any we have seen since we left the Black Hills. When we got to the top it rained and hailed very hard and turned very cold suddenly. Doctor and I were out in most of the storm, as we had strayed too far from the wagons. Emcamp on a little stream, do not know the name. See a few Indians of the Snake tribe. See a few strange flowers, very pretty. Very poor grass. Very cold at night. Made 18 miles.

So many thousands of wagons passed this way that even the sage brush doesn't grow in the ruts. Scene is in western Wyoming, 1987.

Monday, Aug. 9. Freezing cold this morning, but as soon as the sun rises it is very warm. Father is much better today. Our road today is very hilly and sandy, but the earth begins to look more fertile. Encamp tonight on Ham's Fork. Here is an Indian village consisting of some 40 or 50 tents covered with buffalo skins. We have plenty of visitors tonight. They are very friendly. Passed 4 graves. Find good grass and a beautiful campground. Made 16 miles.

Tuesday, Aug. 10. Wind south. Pleasant. Conclude to stay here till noon to rest our cattle. Find plenty of gooseberries, they are very sour and smooth. We do a little washing here. We caught some speckled trout. Had a very high mountain to climb. Encamped in a

Rail ⟶

Every grave along the Oregon Trail is important because in it
are remains of someone who was loved. Probably one of the best
kept graves is that of Rebecca Burdick Winters. She died of
cholera on August 15, 1852. When the Burlington Railroad sur-
veyed for its main line across Nebraska the grave was in the
direct line of the route. To preserve the lonely little grave
on the plains, the railroad changed its route thus the track
passes the grave by about twelve feet on the south. The
original marker was just the metal tire from a wagon wheel
which remains to this date, but a carved granite monument has
been added. The area is fenced with iron pipe. Folklore says
that old-timer engineers on the passing trains blow the whis-
tle in salute saying,"She came first in this desert wide;
Rebecca...holds the right of way." Hundreds of members of the
Oregon-California Trails Association visited the grave during
a recent convention at nearby Scotts Bluff.

beautiful grove of poplars. Good grass. Made
8 miles.

Wednesday Aug. 11. Wind west. Cool and
pleasant. Get an early start this morning.
I have the toothache today. Roads very moun-
tainous. Passed 10 graves in 2 days. Encamped
on Bear River. Good grass. Willows for fuel.
Made 18 miles. Passed through a beautiful
grove of firs. Find some pretty flowers.

Thursday, Aug. 12. Traveled on till noon
and then stopped to repair our wagon. Have
some very high hills to climb. Good grass.
Passed a station. Met some packers from Oregon.
Find wild flax, red, yellow and black currents,
narrow dock and cranebill and wild pieplant
[rhubarb]. Made 8 miles today.

Friday, Aug. 13. Wind west. Very sultry in
the valleys, but cool on the mountains. Come
to another station. Here is 2 bridges, and
by going over them we can take a cutoff saving
7 miles of very bad mountains. Have to pay $1
per wagon. See some Indians. Have plenty of
good water. Some beautiful springs. Took a
new road leading on the banks of the river.
It is 2 miles farther, but saves some very
high mountains. Passed 2 graves. Encamped
on the river. Made 20 miles.

Saturday, Aug. 14. Very pleasant this morning. Find a berry resembling the whortle-
berry, rather larger. Here we met a man that
had groceries and potatoes to sell at 12 1/2
cents per pound. Of course we bought some,
the first we have seen since we left the
States. They were brought from Salt Lake.
He had butter to sell at 40 cents, and cheese
at 50 cents, and whiskey at 10 shillings a pint.

The grass hoppers are so thick that they look like snow in the air, coming very fast. We can get a good pair of moccasins for $1. Travel on the river bottom most of the day. Made 16 miles.

Sunday, Aug. 15. Sun very pleasant. Can see snow on the mountains. Find an apple that looks like a rosebud, are not good. Passed a beautiful spring. Find good grass. Passed 2 graves. Encamped tonight at Soda Springs.

[Parthenia] These consist of springs of water of an alkaline taste bubbling up through the rock and forming mounds of the mineral from 2 to 20 feet high and with bases of proportional size and gas sufficient coming up to keep them constantly boiling like a pot and the opening at the top resembles a large kettle. Some are very cold and others less so. The water, sweetened and mixed with acid, makes a beautiful effervescing draught. We saw some 10 or 12 scattered over a surface of less than 1/2 mile square. In somr places it boils up in the bed of the river. Made 18 miles.

Monday, Aug. 16. This morning we passed one of those springs about a mile from the camp, which has received the name of the Steamboat Spring. Here the gas rises with such force as to throw the water some 18 inches above the ground. Here we find a great many mounds which have edidently been thrown up by the water, but have been cracked open and are now dry. We left the track of the Californians today for good about 6 miles from the springs. Crossed a chasm in the rocky road, how long, we could not tell, and in places so deep we could not see the bottom. Must have been caused by an earthquake. About a mile from the road saw the crater of an old volcano. Stopped at noon near another soda spring. Found a trading station at the Steamboat Spring. Had a beautiful, level road all day. Crossed some beautiful mountain streams and fine springs. Encamped for the night on a small stream. Made 20 miles.

Tuesday, Aug. 17. Found good, level road for about half the day. Crossed 2 small streams and found trading stations at each. Then came to the dividing ridge between Snake and Bear Rivers and had some pretty hard hills to climb up and down. Upon these hills we found a great many serviceberries, very good to eat. Found 2 of the finest springs we ever saw. Encamped for the night in a valley among the mountains upon a very rapid little stream. Grass good. Made 21 miles.

Wednesday, Aug. 18. Started again down the mountain. A good many steep pitches, but on the whole road very good. Followed down the stream on which we were last night toward Snake River. Found some fine chokecherries today very large. Encamped at night on the same stream. Grass not very good. Here we fell in with another company of 6 wagons mostly from Illinois with Mr. [Benjamin S.] Hyland [from] Plainfield, [Illinois] the captain. [Mr. Hyland, with 2 sons, Amos and Burnham went to Oregon but his divorced wife, Abigail, stayed in Illinois.] As we are just on the borders of the Digger Indians' territory, both companies thought best to increase our strength by combining our forces. We now have 14 wagons in our company and 32 effective men, and keep a guard of 4 men at night, and each man has to stand guard half the night every fourth night. We are now in the valley of the Snake River.

Made 20 miles.

Thursday, Aug. 19. Today came to Fort Hall on
Snake River and passed it at one in the afternoon. It is made of unburnt bricks and is
little larger than a good sized barn. It is
not now occupied by the soldiers, but is used
for a trading station. Some 50 or 100 wagons,
marked "U.S." in large letters stand there
rotting. Encamped about 2 miles from the fort
on Pannock Creek and had very good feed. Made
14 miles.

Friday, Aug. 20. Today we crossed the creek
and came to the Port Neuf River, 2 miles.
This is a stream of considerable size, and we
had to raise our wagon boxes to cross it. All
the streams we have seen since we crossed the
Missouri River have been rapid and, indeed, all
since we crossed the Mississippi, but those on
this side of the mountains are more so, but the
Snake River is the most rapid one I ever saw
for so large a one. It runs over a rock bottom,
and every now and then taking an offset of some
3 to 10 feet in the course of a few rods.
Traveled down the river all day and could see
plenty of good feed nearly all the way, but
were afraid to put our cattle upon it for the
alkali water in the bottom. Made 25 miles.
Did not camp till near sunset, when we found
a good spring and plenty of grass.

Saturday, Aug. 21. Did not exactly like our
camping place, and concluded to go on a few
miles and find a better place and stay over
Sunday. Today we passed the American Falls,
where the river falls about 50 feet in 15 rods.
It is about 20 rods across at this place.
Captain Hyland went before to find grass and
a good place for the Sunday camp. After trav-

eling about 15 miles on the road without feed for our cattle we started out ourselves for grass, and found some very good about half a mile from the road and stopped for the night, while his company followed on about 5 miles and encamped without grass. In the morning[...].

Sunday, Aug 22. Started on and traveled about 2 miles and found them encamped for Sunday on Fall River a very rapid little stream full of little galls of from 2 to 10 feet. Found good bunch grass on the hills. Here we stayed the rest of the day. From the time we crossed the dividing ridge between Bear and Snake Rivers the soil or surface has changed. Hitherto it has been composed mostly of coarse sand but now it has a mixture of clay with it and when tramped up by the numerous teams and wagons, makes the most beautiful cloud of dust you ever saw. Many times it is so thick you cannot see 10 feet and you have to shut your eyes and go it blind. Made 12 miles.

Monday, Aug. 23. Today got rather a late start and traveled over to Raft Creek a distance of 9 miles found rather poor feed. Made 9 miles.

Tuesday, Aug. 24. Got a pretty early start, as we had to travel 15 miles without water or grass. Had a very rough road over rocks varying from the size of a piece of chalk up to a fence block, and so thick that they kept the wagon constantly upon the jump. Dust very troublesome. Killed a black-tailed rabbit. His ears and tail about 6 inches long. A terrible howling of the wolves last night. Grass all fed off, except in the slough. Cattle did very well. Made 11 miles.

Wednesday, Aug. 25. North wind. Traveled on

over a middling-smooth road down the creek to
Snake River and thence to Goose Creek where we
expect to find grass but were disappointed for
it was all bare except sage brush. But we
found a notice left there by some emigrant that
about 3 miles ahead 1/2 mile from the road on
the river there was plenty of grass. Proceeded
there and found it so. Did not arrive till
after sunset. Put our cattle out to feed, and
let them feed till about 9 o'clock, then brought
them into the corral. Made 21 miles.

Thursday, Aug. 27. Today we started on again.
Had a very dusty and rough road till noon, when
we reached the river again and gave our cattle
water, but found no grass. We then went on to
Cut-Rock Creek, but found it dry, or nearly so.
Proceeded up it about 2 miles and found a hole
where there was some water. Took some in our
cans and proceeded up about a mile farther and
found good grass, considering, and camped for
the night. Did not put our cattle in corral,
but let them feed and guarded them outside, as
it was long after dark when we camped. Made
25 miles.

Saturday, Aug. 28. Concluded to stay another
day as we learn from our guide that we are to
have very hard feed for the next 70 miles.
Proceeded up the creek for about 3 miles for
the sake of water. Here we found it coming
out from between the mountains, quite a stream,
but soon sinks away in the sand. Killed 2
black-tailed rabbits. Country generally very

sterile and sandy and a great many rocky hills.
For the last week we have found a great many
dead cattle and the irons of a great many many
wagons, the wood work having been used for fuel.
Timber is very scarce, very little except willow.
Wild sage constitutes much of our fuel. The

river runs over a rocky bed and in most places
has a high steep rocky bank. Our 3 miles today
don't count. Found a company here partly from
Chicago who had lain here 3 days for the sake
of finding 4 horses they had lost, probably
taken by the Indians. They did not guard them
and they [were] missing in the morning. Today
one of them returned alone, and, taking the
back track, the men found the tracks of Indians
who had followed him as far as they dared. Two
of their men went forward to Rock Creek in
search of the horses and were threatened with
an attack by Indians, who came out of the willows, some of them armed with rifles, and made
an attempt to separate them, but did not suc-
ceed, and no shots were fired.

Sunday, Aug. 29. Remain today also. Have a
sermon from Captain Hyland who is a Methodist
preacher. Feed is not very good, but fear we
shall have worse before we have better. Had
a good sing today. [Parthenia does not make
comment but can we assume Cecelia played hymns
on her accordian as part of the simple trail-side
worship service?]

Monday, Aug. 30. Today started for Rock Creek
and had to retrace our 3 miles we traveled
up stream and 9 miles more. Last night we
guarded our cattle out 3 miles from camp on
account of feed. Had 7 men out on guard with
the cattle and 2 at camp. The guard at camp
shot an Indian dog and heard and saw other
signs of Indians. Supposed they came to steal
the Captain's horse, but he was not there.
Made 9 miles.

Tuesday, Aug. 31. Traveled down Rock Creek 12
miles. Found good feed and concluded to stay
till near night tomorrow, and then start out
the long pull of 35 miles at least without

grass, and 22 without water, which we intend to
travel, in part at least, in the night. Road
very dusty and some rock, mostly level, for we
follow the valley of the Snake. The grass we
found on Cut Creek was a kind of coarse grass
as high as your head, nearly, and has a head
on it like blasted wheat. What we have found
on this so far has been bunchgrass, dried as
thoroughly as any hay, and our cattle eat it

Wednesday, Sept. 1. Our cattle are well filled
and in as good order as possible for the trip
across the desert. Crossed Rock Creek about
4 o'clock and started on our way. Passed down
the creek about 5 miles, where there was a poor
chance to get water, but we had supplied ourselves before leaving our last camp. Traveled
on till after dark, and then halted till the
moon arose, about 9 o'clock, and then started
on again. Road in many places very rough and
rocky and all the way dusty, but the dust not
nearly so bad at night as in the day time.
Weather very cold, ao that a man could not
keep warm in walking without an overcoat, and
my hands fairly suffered with the cold. Came
near the river once in the night, but it was
down a dreadful hill and we did not go to it.
Just at sunrise we again came to the river,
down a very steep hill, but there we found no
grass and our cattle had kept so cool they
were not very dry. Rested here about 2 hours
with a good relish, and it is hearty food. For
the last 3 days the weather has appeared like
the closing days of autumn in Illinois. Have
had very warm days generally and very cold
nights, which makes it hard at times for the
guard at night. Rock Creek has very high,
steep rocky banks, and in the course of the
12 miles we have traveled we have found only
2 places where a wagon could cross it. Made
12 miles.

and got our breakfast and started on in search
of grass. Passed down the bottom with high,
rocky banks on each side, nearly perpendicular.
Came to Salmon Creek in about 3 miles, but
found no grass. Here is a fall in the river
about equal to that of the American falls.
Passed on half a mile over a bluff to the
river again. Here we found a company with
whom we were some acquainted, who had been here
2 days and had put their cattle over the river
and found good grass, and said they had been
on before 7 miles to the commencement of the
next desert of 33 miles, and found no grass,
which would make us 40 miles more, but that
is too much for our cattle. It is dangerous
crossing the river, and they had drowned one
horse and one ox putting them over, but it is
the only chance, and so we put them over and
made a boat of one of the wagon boxes to ferry
ourselves over all safe.

Thursday, Sept. 2. Arrived here about noon
and concluded to remain the rest of the day
and tomorrow and recruit. Find very good
bunchgrass and some bottom grass. Two large
springs break out from the side of the mountain
within 1 mile of each other, at least 100 feet
above the river and contain enough water to
turn any mill in Kane County [Illinois] and
dash down with great velocity to the river.
Made 32 miles.

Friday, Sept. 3. Today stayed at camp most of
the day. Tried fishing some, but did not make
out much. Weather very warm. Can see plenty
of large salmon jumping out of the water, but
can't catch them.

Saturday, Sept. 4. This morning we brought
our cattle over again without an accident and

prepared for the long pull. In 3 miles we
passed some hot springs in the river bank and
came to Bannack Creek, but found no grass, but
found a notice that 5 miles below was a ferry
across the river and plenty of grass on the
other side. Went to it, about 1 mile out of
our way, and the ferryman recommended the route
as so much shorter and better supplied with
grass and water that we concluded to try it.
The ferry consists of 2 wagon boxes lashed
together so as to make a boat, and a rope
stretched across the river to pull it across,
and all they asked was $3 a wagon for ferrying.
The day was so windy that we could not cross
so we had to stay on this side and swim out
cattle across the river. Found good grass
about half a mile back. We have had some heavy
sandy roads today, the first for some time.
Made 8 miles. Here we find some Indians with
some very nice salmon for sale and we all got
a good supply. They will trade them for powder, lead, caps, bread, beads, brass nails,
old shirts, or almost anything you have, and
they seem to have a great many. Just below the
ferry is another great falls. Just above, on
the opposite bank, very large springs break
out, high up in the bank, and fall into the
river with a great noise. A fine sight.

Sunday, Sept. 5. No wind this morning and we
ferried over in good season and proceeded on
our way. A few rods below the ferry is another
salmon falls in the river of some 20 feet where
the Indians catch their salmon in traps. Found
very rough rocky road for the first mile then
deep heavy sand for 5 more when we came to a
good sized creek in a deep valley with plenty
of grass and encamped. Here are some 5 or 6
large springs breaking out high up in the rocky
bank and running down, part of the time above

ground and part of the time below, till they
reach the creek, which is very rapid. The water
of this spring and creek has a greenish tint,
but otherwise is perfectly clear and the finest
looking water I ever saw, and tasted good, but
not very cold. The scenery for the last 3 days
has been truly delightful, and only wants a
soil, and what grows on a soil, to make it one
of the most beautiful spots on the earth.
Within these 3 days mill sites enough for the
whole state of Illinois, and finer than I ever
saw there. About a mile from us is the river
and another great fall. The Indians bring us
salmon again, but find dull sale, for we are
all supplied and the market is glutted. Made
6 miles.

Monday, Sept. 6. Had a steep, rocky hill to
climb this morning to start with, then came to
sand again, which lasted 8 miles to another
creek, very heavy road. Here the water falls
down into a very narrow chasm some 40 feet and
runs along it for half a mile or more, dashing
and foaming as it goes. A fine sight. Here
we watered our cattle and then proceeded on
about a couple of miles, where we found grass
and stopped for dinner, then proceeded on, and
did not find water till long after dark, when
we came to a small creek. Watered our cattle
and put them into corral without any feed.
Some Indians camped on the same stream. Made
24 miles.

Tuesday, Sept. 7. This morning found plenty
of excellent bunchgrass on the hills near camp
and let our cattle feed, then started and traveled down the stream about 7 miles and stopped
for dinner, then passed over the hills about
10 miles without water, when we came to the
same creek again, and encamped for the night.

Have found plenty of bunchgrass all the way today, and sage of an enormous size. The general appearance of the country has been more like living than we, have seen for the last thousand miles. Have seen 14 graves in a week. Made 17 miles.

Wednesday, Sept. 8. Traveled over hills again about 8 miles to a dry creek, but some little water standing in puddles. Here we stopped and took dinner. Plenty of dry bunchgrass all the way. After noon we started again and passed up a very rocky hill 3 1/2 miles and most of the way was steep, when we came upon a level tableland and went about 3 miles more over a very rough road, when we came to another dry creek in a ravine with steep, rocky banks. Here we encamped for the night. Find no good water, and but little of it. Plenty of dry willows for fuel. Made 15 miles.

Thursday, Sept. 9. Proceeded over a very tough road to another dry creek, about 6 miles. Here we came upon the road leading from the ferry, 3 miles farther on. Came to a fine stream and cold spring, and several places, some 10 feet across, where water and mud boil up through the sand. Stopped here for dinner and had pretty good grass. Here we found 10 graves, all in a row. All had died from the 28th of July to the 4th of August. Disease unknown. About 7 miles farther on we came to another stream from springs and stopped for the night. Found plenty of grass about 1 mile below on the stream. Made 16 miles.

Friday, Sept. 10. Traveled about 8 miles to a stream of very black water and high colored. Were afraid of it and did not let our cattle drink. About a mile farther on came to a num-

ber of large boiling hot springs, which made
a stream 2 feet wide and 3 or 4 inches deep.
Water very clear and not bad tasting. Here we
stopped and fed our cattle, but did not let
them drink. Traveled along the foot of the
mountains about 5 miles to another creek and
stopped for the night. Plenty of dry bunchgrass. No timber, but willows and sage. Found
8 graves here. Made 15 miles.

Saturday, Sept. 11. Came to another small creek
in about 2 miles, then found no more water
for 8 miles more, when we came to Charlotte
Creek down in valley with steep rocky banks.
The road for the last 3 days has been mostly
very rough and rocky, but generally level, and
the dust has been troublesome. This dust dif-
fers from sand in being mostly clay and is
mixed up by the teams to the depth of from 2
to 4 inches and as light as flour and under it
a hard bottom so that a wagon runs very well
on it where there are no stones in the way, but
there is such a perfect cloud of dust arising
constantly that it almost suffocates our cattle
and is disagreeable to us, and we cannot keep
anything clean. We find plenty of dry bunchgrass all the way, but no green feed have we
had for some time. Our present position must
be high above the river, for we have not come
down much since we climbed the long hill. All
the living creatures we see are a few ravens
and black-tailed rabbits, and flies and white
gnats, and at night we hear some wolves. Here
we found tolerably plenty of dry grass from 1
to 2 miles back on the hills. Concluded to
stay over Sunday. Plenty of willow for fuel
and some Balm of Gilead. Made 10 miles.

Monday, Sept. 13. Today we started again and
had rough, rocky and dusty road along the foot

of the mountains on our right for about 5 miles, then came to light sand and gravel, where the road was hard and smooth. About noon we came to a deep, broad valley, covered with dry grass, as well as the hills that bound it, and so thick as to exclude the sage brush. Begins to look like living, but our cattle are beginning to be tired of dry grass. Here we found a dry creek and some poor water. Traveled on till we came to a small spring. Had very scanty supply of water and it soon got roily [*sic*.]. Hard case, land covered with dry grass. Looks like large wheat field. Made 14 miles.

Tuesday, Sept. 14. Traveled over hilly road of sand and gravel. In about 2 miles we came to a small stream in a deep ravine. Water sinks away in the sand for a few rods, then in about 5 miles more we came to White Horse Creek. Here we watered our cattle and drove on about 2 miles and fed. Then traveled on about 10 miles to another small spring, rather worse case than the other, and stopped for the night. We have no trouble for grass, such as it is. Roads smooth, but hilly. Made 16 miles.

Wednesday, Sept. 15. Today we traveled up a long hill some 4 miles. Road good, ascent very gradual. When we arrived at the top we got a grand view of the Boise River Valley. It is all filled or covered with dry grass and a few trees immediately along the bank, the first we have seen for more than a month. We traveled for some 4 miles on a high, level plain, then came down a steep hill of about 200 feet to another equally level plain, on which we traveled about 3 miles, then took another offset of about 100 feet, and in about a mile and a half came to another offset of about the same height, and we were nearly on a level with the

river. This is a fine, clear stream, and there
are plenty of Indians scattered along its banks.
They bring us a great meny salmon trout, but
no salmon. We have seen no fish since the day
after we left the ferry till now, and we are
getting hungry for some. These Indians have a
great many fine ponies, and most of them have
guns and ammunition, and many of them have almost a complete suit of clothes, which they
have got of the emigrants. They will trade a
very good pony for a good rifle or a coat.
Our company traded 2 guns for 2 ponies. Last
night we had a very heavy wind all night and
it sprinkled slightly for about half a minute,
the first rain we have had since time imme-
morial. On the other side of the river are
lofty, rolling mountains. Made 14 miles.

Thursday, Sept. 16. Traveled down the river.
In about 3 miles we ascended to platform No.
2, and traveled on a good, level road on it
nearly all day, then came down to the river.
These offsets are about as steep as sand and
gravel can be laid without mortar. Road
pretty dusty most of the day. Saw the most
rabbits today that I ever saw in the same
length of time. Frank shot 18 in about an
hour. Tonight we have plenty of good, green
grass for our cattle. Indians bring fish and
rabbits. Made 15 miles.

Friday, Sept. 17. Some traders who are camped
about 2 miles above came down and bought some
of our lame and wornout cattle. Traveled down
the bottom. Road sandy in many places, and
begin to find some sage again. Camped on the
river. Made 13 miles.

Saturday, Sept. 18. Proceeded down the river.
Road sandy and very dusty in places. A great

deal of greasewood and some sage. Country looks about as desolate as ever. About 4 o'clock we crossed Boise River. Very good ford. This river is skirted with timber all the way, consisting of cottonwood, willow and Balm of Gilead. Large quantities of Balm might be procured here. Camped on the river. Had good feed and fuel. Made 15 miles.

Sunday, Sept. 19. Thought we would just drive down to the fort, as we thought it could not be fore than 5 miles. Drove all day but did not see it. Camped about sunset on the river. Saw more fish in the river today than I ever saw before. Made 16 miles.

Monday, Sept. 20. Today we drove down to the fort, about 4 miles. Crossed the ferry, paid $3 a wagon, and spent the rest of the day opposite Fort Boise. It is built of unburned brick, a large yard enclosed by a wall some 12 feet high and 2 buildings of the same about 14 feet square each and 1 story high. It is tenanted by a rough-looking Scotchman and a few Indians and squaws. [Editor's note: The "Scotchman" was Archibald McIntyre.] It is a station of the Hudson's Bay Company. A great many depended on getting provisions here, but failed entirely of getting anything except fish. There is a little sugar for sale here at 75 cents per pound. Prospects seem to darken around us a good deal, for some families are already entirely out of bread, and many more will be in the course of 1 or 2 weeks. We had enough to last us through, but we shall have to divide, if necessary.

Tuesday, Sept. 21. Today Mr. McMillen, Mr. Stowell and Mr. Raymond left us to pack their way through to The Dalles, in company with 11

others from our company. They have 3 ponies
among them, which carry the most of their provisions. They expect to make the trip, 300
miles, in 10 days, while it will probably take
our teams, in their present condition, at least
20 days, and perhaps more. Had some difficulty
in finding our cattle this morning, as we do
not keep a guard over them now, for we are not
much afraid of the Indians stealing them.
Found them about noon and started them on the
way. Had first-rate green feed for them last
night. Proceeded about 5 miles against an in-
creasing west wind, over a very dusty road,
till it became so bad that we could not see
our teams and could hardly breathe, and were
then obliged to heave to for a season. After
awhile the wind shifted more into the north
and blew the dust across the road and then we
proceeded on. Followed up a deep ravine about
3 miles more and encamped for the night without
water or grass. Plenty of sage. Cold. Made
8 miles.

Wednesday, Sept. 22. Started early and followed
up the same ravine to the summit, and then
followed another one down to Malheur River
(the most sluggish stream I have ever seen)
for some time. Here we found but poor feed,
but thought it best to stay for the rest of
the day, as the next stopping place was too
far distant to reach today. Find plenty of
willows. Water not very good. Made 9 miles.

Thursday, Sept. 23. Today we traveled over a
smooth, level road for about 15 miles, when we
came to a sulphur spring. Here we watered our
cattle, but did not find much grass. Country
very poor. Nothing but sage and greasewood.
From the spring we began to ascend hills, and
the country began to improve. Hills mostly

covered with dry grass. Traveled till after
dark without finding water. Camped in valley
among hills. Plenty of thrifty sage. Plenty
dry grass. Tied our cattle to sagebrush. Mr.
Miller thought he saw a bear in the night.
The last 3 nights have been very cold. Made
22 miles.

Friday, Sept. 24. After giving our cattle time
to feed we started. In about a mile we came
to Birch Creek. Water not very good, does not
run more than half the way about the surface.
Stands in pools, tastes of sulphur. In about
4 miles more over the hills we came to Snake
River for the last time. Here it runs between
lofty and inaccessible mountains, so farewell,
Snake. Traveled over high mountains to Burnt
River, 4 miles. Here we stopped and fed our
cattle on dry grass. They are getting tired
of it, for it is too dry. This river is fine,
clear water, about 20 feet wide on an average,
and flows between very lofty mountains, with
just room to pass. Traveled up its bank about
4 miles and encamped. Plenty of dry grass.
Made 13 miles.

Saturday, Sept. 25. Today crossed the river 3
times in going 5 miles, and climbed over high
bluffs the most of the rest of the way. Soon
left the river banks and traveled over bluffs
very hilly for about 6 miles to a small creek
and stopped for the night. Find very little
sage or greasewood. Dry grass. Traveled
12 miles.

Sunday, Sept. 26. Traveled down the creek to
the river 2 miles, here the mountains are so
high and so close that they leave no room for
bluffs and when they close down upon us on one
side of the river our only alternative is to
flee to the other. Crossed the river 5 times

in about 6 miles. These mounts are as near as
I can judge about 1,200 feet high on an average
and as steep as they know how to be. Mostly
covered with dry grass, except where it is
burnt off. See a good many fine fish, but
can't catch them. Today we found a place where
there were a good many green rushes and a good
many birch trees. Here we stopped for the rest
of the day. Made 8 miles. The river bottom
at this place is some 60 rods wide, covered
with timber, as is the bottom most of the way.
Birch, cottonwood and willow and some Balm of
Gilead, a few scattering pines and cedars on
the mountain high above us. Scenery fine.
[Editor's note: The "Balm of Gilead" was a
cottonwood tree, the most important tree on
the Oregon Trail because it was noted for its
fragrance when spring buds blossomed and was
then only shade tree to be found for almost
1,000 miles.]

Monday, Sept. 27. Today we crossed the river
for the last time (9 times in all) about half
a mile from camp and started up a small creek,
very rapid. Got up the hill pretty fast by
following it. Crossed it 9 times in going 4
miles, then turned from it up to another small
stream and spring. Here we watered our cattle
and drove up another steep hill and stopped to
feed on some bunchgrass. The grass along here
has been mostly burned off and we have to get
it where we can catch it. Drove down the hill
and found a spring brook, which we followed
down for some 2 miles, then crossed over a
ridge to another creek and soon came again
near Burnt River and camped on it. Grass
good. Some packers overtook us from behind,
hurrying on to procure provisions. They give
a sad account of the destitution of those who
are behind. Say there are but few who have

more than 5 days' provisions. Made 14 miles.

Tuesday, Sept. 28. This morning met some traders from Oregon, buying lame cattle. River forks some little distance above camp and we take the right-hand fork. Followed it up all day among hills and camp on it at night. Made 10 miles.

Wednesday, Sept. 29. Cross the stream twice, then leave it and follow up a small creek to a spring and water our cattle, as we are to travel 18 miles without water. Traveled over hills till afternoon, then came to a pretty level piece of land covered with sage, on which we traveled till near night, and then descended to another beautiful smooth plain several miles in extent, bounded by the Blue Mountains, beautiful in the distance and covered with pine. Looks as though we were coming somewhere. Camped among the sage without water. Plenty of grass for our cattle on hill near by. Made 18 miles.

Thursday, Sept. 30. After going about 4 miles we found a kind of dry creek, where there was plenty of water standing in pools, but poor stuff. Here we watered our cattle. Drove on about 5 miles and got badly fooled by the willows growing abundantly here, about 2 miles to the left, as we supposed it was Powder River. Stopped on some good feed for our cattle and looked there for water to get our dinner, but found nothing but dirty pools. The soil on this plain is much better than we have seen before. Grass in many places fresh and abundant. In about a mile's travel we came to a small stream, a branch of Powder River, very sluggish. Water poor, bad ford, and in about 6 miles more came to one of the main branches of the Powder River and stopped

for the night. Found good grass and fine
water. Found more Oregon traders here. They
say we must hurry if we get over the Blue Mountains. Rains some in the valley and snows
on the mountains. Very cold all day. Made
15 miles.

Friday, Oct. 1. Let our cattle feed till
afternoon. One of the packers we had seen
before came back. Had been on to the Grand
Ronde and bought 50 pounds of flour for $30,
and was hurrying back to the relief of his
friends. Traveled about 2 miles down the
stream, then crossed it and in about 5 miles
crossed another branch of Powder River, fine
stream. Then crossed several small streams
and ascended to a high tableland and went about
6 miles upon it before finding water. Nearly
dark when we camped on a small stream. Water
not very good. Grass tolerable. No wood but
green willows. Very cold. Rained some in
fore part of the day. Plenty of snow to be
seen on the mountains. Roads good, no dust,
the first time we have been free from it for
a long time. Have seen 35 graves since leaving
Fort Boise. Made 12 miles.

Saturday, Oct. 2. Could not raise fire enough
to cook breakfast. Powerful cold. Started
early and in about 3 miles came to foot of
mountain. Climbed the mountain. Ascent very
gradual, about 3 miles, when we came to a fine
little valley with some springs in it and
plenty of grass. Followed up it about a mile
and then up the mountain 2 miles, when we came
in sight of the Grand Ronde, a beautiful, level
valley, nearly round, I should think, and some
15 miles in diameter, but O! the getting down
to it over a long, steep and stony hill, is
equal to any getting downstairs I ever saw,

and I have seen some on this road. Arrived
at the bottom and found feed had been mostly
burned off, but found enough for our cattle.
Here we found another trading station from
Oregon. They sell flour for 60 cents per
pound, salt at 50 cents, and first-rate fat
beef, which they brought with them or drove,
at 20 to 25 cents. Stopped and fed and then
traveled on about 5 miles to a spring and then
camped. Good water and grass, but no wood,
except a kind of green stuff that won't burn
nohow. Still cold, and freezes considerably.
Did not get very near any snow nor too much
timber. The traders say they drove their beef
cattle from The Dalles in 8 days. The soil of
this valley is fine. Made 18 miles.

Sunday, Oct. 3. Have not seen any of the
clover spoken of by others, but have found
plenty of red-top grass, both here and on
Powder River, and it grows very thrifty. The
Indians have all left for their winter quar-
ters. Traders say they were very thick here
about 2 weeks ago, and are said to be very
rich in ponies, and traded a good many of
cows. Considerably civilized. Raise some cattle
and some vegetables for sale, but they did not
leave much marks of civilization on the road
or near it that could be seen. Traveled along
the west side of the valley at the foot of the
mountains about 3 miles, when we came to a
small stream and then commenced ascending the
mountain, very steep in many places, and con-
tinues to ascend for about 6 miles. A very
hard drive, but at the top found the grass
burned off and there was no water, so had to
go on till we came to Grand Ronde River, 10
miles. Worst hill to go down that we have yet
found, long, steep, and rocky. Our road today
has been mostly lofty pines as far as I ever

saw, and tonight we have plenty of dry pine
for fires. The feed here has been very
thoroughly fed off, but we found plenty on the
mountain side, among the pines. This river
runs through the middle of the Grand Ronde,
a fine little stream, rapid and shallow. Made
15 miles.

Monday, Oct. 4. This morning got a late start
and commenced climbing again. Very steep hill
to start with and about a mile long, then had
hills to ascend and descend all day, many of
them steep. About night found a place where
we could find some standing water about half
a mile from the road, down a very steep hill
all the way. Poor stuff, but it was the best we
could do. Camped and turned our cattle out to
grass, but did not drive them down to water, as
it was almost dark   Plenty of pine. Today saw
2 very small black squirrels. Made 15 miles.

Tuesday, Oct. 5. Stayed till near noon and
let our cattle feed. The grass is very good
and quite fresh in many places among the pines.
We find pine, spruce, tamarack and fir here.
Doctor Miller's company from Iowa are here,
entirely out of flour. Have some loose cattle
which they kill now and then for food. Traded
them some flour for beef, sold them some and
loaned them some to be repaid at The Dalles.
Hard times. Many cattle are failing and all
are very poor and a good many get lost among
the thick timber. A good many wagons are left,
some broken and some good and sound, because
the cattle are not able to take them along.
So much good pine here, they do not burn them.
The general appearance of the country is alto-
gether changed. The soil, even on the mountains, is quite good, and in the valleys it
is excellent. In many places the road has to

twist around a good deal among the trees.
Traveled on about 7 miles on a mountain ridge,
sometimes on one side, sometimes on the other,
pretty sidling in places. Do not have to rise
and fall as many notes as common today. Begin
to hope we are getting out of the mountains.
Camped on the mountain. A good spring about
a quarter of a mile off, down at the foot of
the mountain. Timber very thick today. Grass
good. Made 7 miles.

Wednesday, Oct. 6. Concluded to rest here today and recruit our cattle, as we have good
feed and they have had a hard pull of it for
the last 4 days. Spent the day in cooking and
hunting for cattle lost in the brush, as a
great many have been lost here.

Thursday, Oct. 7. Today stayed till about noon
and then started on about 6 miles to another
spring, still in the thick timber, very thick.
Find plenty of good grass all the way. Made
6 miles.

Friday, Oct. 8. Started for the Umatilla River.
Roads slightly descending nearly all the way,
and in some places steep. At last came in sight
of the valley, covered entirely with dry grass,
except a small skirt of timber along the river,
and literally dotted with Indian ponies and
cattle. Commenced the descent into the valley
very gradual, said to be 5 miles down hill.
Don't think it was much overrated. The grass
here is very poor, having been fed off by the
ponies and cattle. Soil excellent. This valley is the headquarters of the Cayuse Indians.
They are more civilized than any we have seen
before. Bought a few potatoes of them. They
are killing some very fat cattle and sell the
beef at 15 to 20 cents per pound. No other

provisions can be had here, and it is a death
blow to the hopes of many hungry people. Found
a man here who had left our company some time
ago and been on to The Dalles and returned with
a pony-load of provisions. Gives a very dis-
couraging account of the prospect before us.
Grass is very poor all the way. No provisions
for sale between here and The Dalles. Made
15 miles.

Saturday, Oct. 9. Our friend from The Dalles
advises us to stay and recruit our cattle, as
we shall have no more as good grass as we have
here, but the prospect here is nothing but
starvation for ourselves and teams. Started
off after noon and went down the river 6 miles,
put our cattle over the bluffs but found poor
feed. Find some prairie chickens. Made
6 miles.

Sunday, Oct. 10. Traveled down river. Passed
over bluffs, some sand. Crossed river and
passed some 7 miles and camped. Find a great
many mice living in holes in the ground. Timber mostly Balm of Gilead, some willow. Made
9 miles.

Monday, Oct. 11. Climbed the bluff, descent
very gradual, but some 3 miles long. After
passing some 7 miles we found good feed, dry
grass, and stopped for noon, then passed on
some 7 miles more and stopped for the night.
No water. Road good. Plenty of dry grass.
Mice very plenty. Made 14 miles.

Tuesday, Oct. 12. Put our cattle down to the
river about 2 miles for drink and got one of
them stuck in the mud. Spent the forenoon in
trying to get him out, but failed. We killed
him. Started on and came to the river in about

74

3 miles and traveled down it in about 3 miles
and we camped on it. Poor feed. Made 6 miles.

Wednesday, Oct. 13. Traveled down 3 miles to
the Indian agency, the first frame house we
have seen since we left the Missouri River,
and they have actually got a stoned-up well.
The agent was gone to The Dalles, but we left
2 of our wagons there and sold 3 cattle to
some traders, and put all the teams to Stephen's
wagon and proceeded. Our loads are light, but
our cattle are getting powerful weak, and we
think best to favor them as much as possible.
An Indian here has some flour for sale at 50
cents per pound. A white man has some corn,
brought from Fort Walla Walla, which he sells
at the rate of 6 pint cupfulls for $1, and it
sells fast. Traveled on about 5 miles, after
crossing the river and leaving it. Road very
sandy, the heaviest I ever saw for so long a
distance. Camped on the open prairie. No
water. Burn greasewood, of which we have seen
a good deal today. Looks familiar, but old-
fashioned. We find it to our advantage to
camp between the watering places on account of
grass. Seventy graves since leaving Fort Boise.
Made 8 miles.

Thursday, Oct. 14. Started on again and traveled over the same heavy sand about 5 miles
more to Alder Creek. A sluggish, dirty stream
with some willows on its banks.

[Cecelia] Here we saw Mr. [William S.] Tor-
rence the Indian Agent, on his way back to his
[place at] Milwaukie, loaded with provisions.
[He] seemed much pleased to see us. Told us
a great deal about James, as he is well acquainted with him. After dinner we started
on. Carried our water with us. Very warm and

sandy. Encamped on the prairie. No wood, nor water for our cattle. Warm nights. Made 11 miles.

Friday, Oct. 15. Looks very much like rain, cool. Frank and the doctor have concluded to start on ahead, as Stephen bought an Indian pony and they will take it and go to The Dalles and there meet us. Encamped at a spring of miserable water. Here we met Mr. Lot Whitcomb, direct from Oregon. Told us a great deal about Oregon. Was well acquainted with James, spoke very highly of him. He has provisions, but not to sell, but gives to all he finds in want and are not able to buy. Took supper and traveled all day. Made 15 miles.

Saturday, Oct. 16. [Mr. Whitcomb had] breakfast with us. Traveled all day over deep sand and dust, and had no water till night. Encamped on Willow Creek. The water stands in holes, but found 3 good springs. Made 18 miles.

Sunday, Oct. 17. Warm and pleasant. Stay here today to rest our teams. Some cedar and willow. See no Indians. Drive our cattle over the bluffs some 3 miles.

[**Parthenia**] Find very poor feed all along here. Here are 12 graves all together. We hope this is the last Sabbath we shall spend on the road.

Monday, Oct. 18. Very cloudy. Started on and it soon began to rain. As we left the creek we had a very long, steep hill to climb. The train we started with are all behind, and we travel alone. At noon it rained very hard and we all got wet, which was very reviving. Pleasant in the afternoon. Road very hilly

all day, and dusty. Camped without wood or
water and with little grass. Made 13 miles.

Tuesday, Oct. 19. Cool and pleasant. High
west wind. Road lay through a deep, narrow
valley, but very barren. At noon we camped by
a small spring coming out of a hill. No grass
here. From here pass over high bluffs and
descend a very steep hill to John Day River,
a very rapid stream. No wood here, except a
few very small willows. Some sage here, which
we burn for fuel. Grass poor. All the country, from the [Umatilla] Indian Agency to
this place, is about as barren and desolate as
any we have passed over, and we have seen
nothing that could be fairly called wood since
we left the Umatilla. Made 13 miles.

Wednesday, Oct. 20. Very pleasant this morning. Our first act was to pass up a very
stony, rocky and sandy hill, as bad as any we
have had, all things considered, and when we
arrived at the top we stopped for dinner. Here
we have good grass, the first since we left
Umatilla. Here the doctor met us on his way
back from The Dalles. Franklin had gone down
by the boat. He brought some flour, pork, salt
and saleratus. Prices are coming down at The
Dalles. Flour can be had at 15 cents, pork at
37 1/2 cents, salt at 25 cents. Afternoon
traveled on about 6 miles and encamped on the
prairie. Plenty of dry grass, but no wood nor
water. Country quite changed. Land all covered
with a fine growth of dry grass. Pretty hills.
Soil good. Made 9 miles.

Thursday, Oct. 21. Traveled on. Road good but
rather hilly. Plenty of grass all the way.
Came to a spring of poor water in about 9 miles
more. Stopped and watered our cattle, but did

not feed. Passed on about 3 miles more and
camped for the night. Grass excellent for dry,
but no water. Made 12 miles.

Friday, Oct. 22. Arose early and drove down
to the great Columbia River for wood and water
for breakfast. Had a very long but not very
steep hill to descend. At the foot we found
a trading station. Sell flour, pork, sugar
and tobacco at 40 cents per pound. Stopped
and got our breakfast. No wood but very poor
willows and some greasewood. Drove on to
Deschutes River, 3 miles. No grass in the
bottoms, all eaten off. The Columbia here is
very rapid and shallow, stream apparently
about the size of Rock River, Illinois, flow-
ing over a rocky bottom, with frequent falls
and not navigable for sap troughs or canoes.
[Editor's note: Sap trough was a log that had
been hollowed out for the collection of sap
from maple trees (maple syrup), these logs
sometimes served as dug-out canoes in emergen-
cies but were highly unstable.] Banks were
very high, steep and rocky and bottom very
narrow, and in some places sandy. Deschutes
River is, to appearances, nearly as large as
The Columbia, but it must be much smaller, and
comes dashing down over the rocks, as rapid as
water can come on a plane inclined 1 foot in
20. Here is a ferry at $2 for those who have
money, and a ford for those who have not. The
latter is the most numerous class. After crossing this river we climbed a very steep and long
hill, but good road, and passed on about a
mile on the level and camped for the night.
Here is a good spring on the hill. Found
rather poor grass, but thought beat to stop
for fear we could not climb the other hill.
Made 7 miles.

Saturday, Oct. 23. Traveled on about 2 miles

and came to another hill as bad as the last.
Hard pull as our cattle are so much weakened,
but it is the last [big hill] we shall have.
Then down a steep hill to Olney's Creek. Here
is a house and a white man (Mr. Olney) living
with a squaw. There are also 2 houses at
Deschutes River, and some tents belonging to
the Walla Walla Indians, who do some ferrying
and act as guides to those who ford. Pretty
shrewd fellows for money, but very civil. From
thence we went over bluffs, ascent and descent
very gradual, to a creek 5 miles from The Dalles,
called Five Miles Creek, and encamped for the
night. Stephen had gone before to The Dalles,
and returned, bringing the intelligence that
Mr. McMillen had returned there with some provisions for us from the [Willamette] Valley.
Remained all night and did some cooking for the
journey down by water. Have long been convinced
that we are too late to cross the Cascade
Mountains [on the Barlow Road] with safety,
so we conclude to leave our cattle and wagon
at The Dalles and proceed down by water. Hire
a man to take care of the cattle at $6 per
head and deliver them in the valley in the
spring as soon as it is safe to travel over
the mountains. Made 9 miles.

Sunday, Oct. 5. Traveled to The Dalles, 5
miles, and found a boat ready to sail. Put
our loads on board and got on ourselves and
were ready to be off. Stephen stayed there
to take care of the cattle and some other business and the rest of us went on. It was an
open-keel boat, rowed by 3 men, and we went
on at a pretty good rate. The appearance of
the river here changes, and from being a rapid,
shallow and narrow stream it becomes a wide,
deep and still one, in some places more than
a mile wide and too deep to be sounded. The

water is clear and fine, and the banks are
precipitous and rocky, and several hundred
feet high in most places. We had a very fa-
vorable run, for the weather was clear and
calm. This is said to be a very windy stream
and the channel being so deep it follows it
up and often prevents boats from running for 3
or 4 days. During the night it rained a good
deal and we got pretty thoroughly wet. About
2 o'clock we hove to, to wait for daylight.
Went on shore and got breakfast. Rained hard
nearly all the time. Here is a narrow bottom
and some Balm of Gilead growing, some of the
trees more than 4 feet in diameter. We are
now only 6 miles from the Cascades. The mountains are covered with a thick growth of lofty
pines and fir, and the pack trail which passes
along here seems almost impassable, the mountains are so very steep. Passed down to the
Cascades, which consist of an immense pile of
loose rocks across the stream, over which the
water runs with great rapidity for 6 miles.

The Indians have a tradition that many years
ago the Columbia ran above here, the same as
above The Dalles, but the mountains got into
a fight and threw large rocks at each other,
which, falling into the river, dammed it up,
and, indeed, the river appears like a vast
millpond. The distance from The Dalles to the
Cascades is 45 miles. Here is a large ware-
house and from it proceeds a railroad 3 miles
long, made of scantling and plank without iron.
On this runs a small car propelled by a mule
attached to it by a long rope for an engine,
and a pair of thills between which the engineer
stations himself and walks and guides the car.
On this the charge is 75 cents per 100 pounds,
but takes no passengers. At the end of the
railroad the goods have to be let down perpen-
dicularly some 150 feet to the river, from

whence they are taken on a boat to the steamboat landing, about 3 miles more. Charge, 75
cents in all. Rained hard most of the day.
Women walked down on land and expected some
goods that night, but could not get them down.
Had no tent, no beds, and no food, except what
we bought. Mr. Miller stayed with the goods
and the rest of us went to the tavern to stay.
The steamer *Multnomah* came up about dark and
stayed until morning. Here we came across Mr.
Stowell, who had been detained by sickness.
Early in the morning Mr. Miller came down with
the goods and we all got on board the steamer.
Charge $6 per passenger. Distance to Portland,
65 miles. The appearance of the river below
the Cascades is about the same as above. Rises
and falls with the tide in the Pacific. Had
a very pleasant ride. Much better than an ox
team, where you have to work your passage by
running on foot. The banks soon began to grow
less steep and high, and soon we were in the
valley, but could see nothing except timber on
shore, but that was fine. Passed some timber
farms and good dwellings and one sawmill belonging to the Hudson's Bay Company. Passed
Fort Vancouver, pleasantly situated on the
north side of the river. About 2 o'clock came
into the Willamette (pronounced Will-am-et)
River, much like the Columbia, being wide,
deep, and slow, and soon were at Portland, the
largest town now in the territory, and a fine
town it is, and would compare favorably with
many eastern cities. At the head of ship nav-
igation, it is bound to be the great commercial
emporium of the northwest. Here we remained
3 days nearly, when Brother James came for us
with his teams and we started with him for his
farm, 10 miles distant. [Editor's note: This
farm was in Washington County near the village
of Reedville which is about-mid-way between
Beaverton and Hillsboro. [‾]

Appendix A

Letter from Dr. William Adams, pioneer of 1852, to George
H. Himes, Oregon Pioneer Association.

Hillsboro, Oregon. June 1, 1905

Dr. Bro. Himes

Since my pleasant interview with you and your kind inquiries concerning one once so dear to me and dearer still as the years roll on
and bear me with them, tenderly, painlessly, joyously, towards the
hour when, by God's grace, I hope to meet her among the inumerable
host of the redeemed.

> Where love hath put off in the land of its birth
> The stains it had gathered in this
> And hope, the sweet singer that gladdens the Earth
> Lies asleep in the bosom of bliss.

And now, 38 years after her death her name is unexpectedly brot
into such prominence I am glad that, with trembling hand I can respond
if not comply with your request for a sketch.

My first acquaintance with Cecelia was when I secured board at her
father's country tavern to begin the practice of Medicine. Her opportunities had been meager tho she was teaching in a district school;
but she siezed upon such opportunities as I could give her with such
eagerness and success that it was a pleasure to help her. And at the
end of a year when I made up my mind to seek another location I found
I couldn't leave her behind, and I soon found she didn't want to be
left.

I was poor and in debt, and in no circumstances to keep a wife
just then; and I told her so; but she said I wouldn't have to keep her.
She would help me more than she would hinder me, even in my practice—
and so she did. Her parents said she was their weakling—didn't know
as she was worth having, but gave her to me. She was a born musician,
Artist and teacher, and worker too, and would have made a success had
she had that sort of man. And when after 3 years she asked me to come
with her to Oregon I had to come. Then her twin sister Mrs. Blank and
her husband—then her father and brother Frank, then my brother Calvin
and his wife who was a cousin of Mrs. Ralph Geer, all concluded to
come, and into the land of Oregon we came, all safer and wiser.

Her twin sister was just like her but very different—taciturn, but
never gloomy, never sang nor played on instruments—had good taste, but
no ambition in art—never taught nor wanted to—steady, earnest, cheerful work—Neither had any children, but she and her husband, (both living) have raised, in whole or in part, ten orphan children, and many
students of Pacific University remember them with affection and gradi-
tude.

"The twins" were always together when circumstances would permit

81

Hillsboro Or. June 1, 1905

Dr. Bro. Hines

Since my pleasant inter
view with you and your kind
inquiries concerning one once so
dear to me and dearer still as
the years roll on and bear me with
them, tenderly, painlessly, joyously, towards the hour when, by God's grace, I
hope to meet her among the innumer-
able host the redeemed,
"Where love hath put off in the land of its birth
"The stains it had gathered in this.
"And Hope, the sweet singer that gladdens the Earth
"Lies asleep in the bosom of bliss.
And now, when 38 years after her death,
her name is unexpectedly brot into
such prominence I am glad that,
with my trembling hand I can respond
& not comply with your request for a
sketch.
My first acquaintance with Cecilia

83

and if they ever disagreed or doubted each other I do not know it. In all the long journey thro the wilderness that, with their husbands, slept at night in the same wagon, Mr. Blank's, walking much of the day, and as the oxen began to weaken, they would walk together all day, sometimes over 20 miles. There were rather short, and, when they took the short steamboat ride from The Cascades to Portland, a lady asked my brother's wife if those little girls' mother was with them.

She died in that sister's home, and in the sightly Buxton Cemetery near Forest Grove, is a beautiful granite monument, erected by Mrs. Blank. One face of which is engraved:

Cecelia Emily McMillan
Wife of Wm Adams
Twin Sister of
Mrs. P.E. Blank

Theirs has been a pious, unselfish, earnest, strenuous life. The sister has now lived just twice as long as she did.

As for me I desire to leave it on record for the glory of God and the encouragement of fellow mortals, living or to live, that now, at 83, I do not find, as the poet Ossian did, that "Age is dark and unlovely." I have lived and still live in a wonderful world, and a wonder to myself, so much so, that, for years, I could not bring myself to believe them real. Such wonderful facilities, such wonderful powers, wonderful surroundings, wonderful needs, wonderful supplies, glorious hopes, fearful responsibilities, large opportunities, mortifying failures, humiliating blunders; but thro it all, study has been a delight, teaching a pleasure, and moderate labor, recreation.

But the strangest, sweetest thing that I have found in life is life itself, with all that it implies—thought—feeling—purpose—affection—ambition —action—duty—destiny.

My precious brother who now cares for me, now 85, often walks two miles to his work, and back again to be with his invalid, aged wife, who has not, however, given up work—while I generally camp upon the field sawing wood, clearing land, fencing, cultivating—whatever a cripple can do to advantage, wielding most implements pretty well, except a pen or spoon or my tongue. We have spent more than half our lives together, have often differed in opinion, but never quarreled —he won't. He has never tasted what Paul so aptly called "the cup of devils," and don't mean to. He has never used tobacco, and I have not, for more than fifty years, and neither of us has ever been a habitual user of tea or coffee or any needless drink. I was once intoxicated, in childhood. Never drink since. He has never indulged a doubt of the precious Gospel—I was a sceptic for many years, but never a scoffer. These facts are not worth telling unless there is a moral to them. We are the wonder of our neighbors for health and ability to labor. He was a weakly boy and I a cripple from birth. We could only wish for greater usefulness, and are not at all pure but the way is already opened for a larger usefulness that we had dared to hope for. However, we rejoice more in our strength and courage than in all the wealth of all the [not intelligible].

(End of letter)

Appendix B

Clippings from
Washington County News
Forest Grove, Oregon.

November 10, 1910, Page 1

CELEBRATE SIXTIETH WEDDING ANNIVERSARY

Mr. and Mrs. Stephen Blank Are Remembered by Relatives.

ARE PIONEER RESIDENTS

Elaborate Dinner Commemorates Happy Event of Sixty Years Ago—Mrs. Ordway Writes Pretty Tribute.

Surrounded by relatives who brought with them the best wishes of their friends from East and West, Mr. and Mrs. Stephen Blank celebrated their sixtieth wedding anniversary at their home, on "A" street, in this city, yesterday afternoon. The occasion was commemorated by an elaborate dinner. Mr. Blank's brother, Harrison Blank, of Winthrop, Iowa, brought gifts and greetings from the eastern friends of the esteemed couple. At the close of the dinner the guests presented Mr. and Mrs. Stephen Blank with a purse containing $60.

Mr. and Mrs. Stephen Blank have lived in Forest Grove continuously since 1852. Both are natives of New York state and were born in 1820.

Among the relatives of the honored couple present were: Mrs. Jane McMillan Ordway, the noted writer of Portland, Mrs. Ella Caufield, of Oregon City, and Mrs. Louise Philip, of Monmouth.

Friends throughout the city also joined in extending many "happy returns of the day" to Mr. and Mrs. Blank.

Washington County News-Times
Forest Grove, Oregon.

December 30, 1915, Page 1

PIONEER WOMAN PASSES TO HER REWARD

Mrs. Parthenia McMillan E. Blank, one of Forest Grove's oldest citizens and earliest settlers, died at her home in this city on Christmas day, aged 86 years.

She was born February 16th, 1829, in New York State. She was married to Stephen Blank, November 9th, 1850. They crossed the plains together from Galena, Ill., in 1852, locating in Forest Grove in 1853, where they have since resided. Mr. Blank passed away about a year ago.

Mrs. Blank had been in poor health for about two or three years, some time since suffering a paralytic stroke from which she never fully recovered.

She was one of the first members of the Congregational church, and was a faithful, active member until incapacitated by paralysis and old age.

The Blanks had no children of their own, but adopted three daughters, whom they raised. Among these were Mrs. J. M. Garrison, of Salem; Mrs. Ida Horner, deceased and Mrs. Emma Allen, of California. She raised several other children, but these were the only adopted ones. The latter included Mrs. S. L. Phillips, who remained faithfully with Mr. and Mrs. Blank during their last illness, patiently caring for their every need.

Mrs. Blank was a sister of the late Captain James McMillan, who died two years ago. He was the first to build a home in Forest Grove, coming here in 1846.

A notable event in the history of the Blank family, was the celebration of their 60th wedding anniversary, November 9th, 1910.

Mrs. Blank was always thoughtful of new-comers and helpful to those in trouble. Truly it can be said of her that "She hath done what she could". She is the last of a family of eight brothers and sisters. Her parents resided for many years before their death in Forest Grove. McMillan's Addition in Portland was named for the family.

For a number of years Mr. and Mrs. Blank kept a hotel in the house which has since been moved farther down on North "A" street and is now owned by John Anderson.

The funeral services were conducted from the Congregational church Monday, December 27th, Rev O. H Holmes, the pastor, officiating. Burial in Buxton Cemetery.

Transcribed from
Hillsboro Argus
Hillsboro, Oregon

March 18, 1919, Page 5

WILLIAM ADAMS

William Adams dies at the home of his great-niece Mrs. Emma Pitman, Friday, March 7 1913, after an illness extending over but a few weeks. He was born at Eden Corner, near Buffalo, N.Y., March 22 1822 and was married to Miss Cecelia McMillan at Elgin, Ill in 1850. In 1852 he and his wife crossed the plains to Oregon.

Mr. Adams was educated at Oberlin College, and was one of the first to take up the higher studies in that institution. He was a graduate in medicine and practiced several years.

He was the last of a family of five brothers, his brother Calvin, dying in 1907 at the age of 87. Mrs. Adams died in February 1867. The funeral took place Sunday, interment being at the Buxton Cemetery by the side of the wife of his youth.

For three years he has been a member of the Pitman household and for years prior to that he had been more or less with his brother, the late Calvin Adams. He was a great believer in out-of-door sleeping and this probably had something to do with his advanced age—nearly 91 years.

84

Bibliography

To assist in locating places, we referred to these maps:

Official road maps of Illinois, Missouri, Iowa, Nebraska,
 Wyoming, Idaho, Oregon.
Reinforcement of place-locations was obtained with
 Goode's World Atlas 12th Ed, 1966
 World Book Atlas 1962

BOOKS

Franzwa, Gregory M. *Maps of the Oregon Trail*. The
 Patrice Press. 1982

Haines, Aubrey L. *Historic Sites Along the Oregon Trail*.
 The Patrice Press. (2nd Ed.) 1985

Mattes, Merrill J. *The Great Platte River Road*.
 Nebraska State Historical Society. 1969

Scott, Leslie M. (Ed.) *History of the Oregon Country*. By
 Harvey W. Scott. The Riverside Press. 1924

Webber, Bert (Ed.) *The Oregon Trail Diary of James Akin,
 Jr. in 1852*. Webb Research Group. 1989.

_____. *The Oregon Trail Diary of Rev. Edward
 Evans Parrish in 1844*. Webb Research Group. 1988

_____. *The Oregon & California Trail Diary
 of Jane Gould in 1862*. Webb Research Group. 1987

Newspapers consulted are cited in Appendix B.

The photographs of scenes along the Oregon Trail were
made by Bert Webber. The pictures of the monuments in
the Mountain View Cemetery and of the family home in
Hillsboro were made by David and Susan Payne. The
publisher thanks them for their interest and help.

Index

Page numbers in *italic* are photographs